Women of the Bible

Their Stories in Verse

JAMES VASQUEZ

Women of the Bible: Their Stories in Verse

Published by Wheatmark®
610 East Delano Street, Suite 104
Tucson, Arizona 85705 U.S.A.
www.wheatmark.com

International Standard Book Number: 978-1-60494-270-5
Library of Congress Control Number: 2009925752

www.WomenoftheBibleinVerse.com

Dedication

This book of poems is dedicated to the women in every land whose courage, wisdom and love have gained for their men and children greater wealth than has ever been counted and richer blessings than have ever been told, who have been content when not recognized for all they have sacrificed every hour of the day. Your reward is due now but will be fully yours only in heaven.

Contents

From the Old Testament

From the New Testament

Acknowledgements

The following poems in this collection have appeared in publications as indicated:

A Canaanite Woman, *Poet's Pen*, Fall 2004

A Widow from Nain, *Poetry Church Collection*, U.K., Summer 2004 Vol. 9

A Widow's Plea, *The Jewish Magazine*, May 2004; *Poet's Pen*, Spring 2003

Hannah's Song, *The Jewish Magazine*, February 2004

Abigail—A Kinder, Happier Fate, *The Jewish Magazine*, January 2004

This Favor Over All, *Poet's Pen*, Fall 2003

A Noble Wife, *The Jewish Magazine*, May 2004; *Poet's Pen*, Summer 2002

Sarah - Mother of Nations, *The Jewish Magazine*, June 2002

Esther, *The Jewish Magazine*, February 2002

Eve, *The Jewish Magazine*, June 2001

Ruth - She Was One of Us, *The Jewish Magazine*, May 2001

Deborah - March on my Soul, *The Jewish Magazine*, April 2001

Two Coins I Bring, *Poet's Pen*, Winter 2001

Martha, *Poet's Pen*, Summer 2000

Mary Magdalene, *Poet's Pen*, Winter 2000

Foreword

Has the world ever known a greater tribute to women than that found in Proverbs 31? Here we see a woman who rises while it is yet dark and is still busy long after sunset, who prepares clothes for her family—thus she can laugh at "the days to come," including cold winter days—treats household servants well and gives to the poor; who engages in business for family's sake, including trading and bringing her goods "from afar" to set a better table; who teaches others wisely and, it seems, in every way brings honor to her husband and children. Thus they praise her and rise to call her blessed. Her husband reaps the benefits of this industrious and devoted woman for when he takes his place among the elders of the city they respectfully acknowledge him. Indeed, her worth cannot be measured even when compared to "many rubies."

But from beginning to end the Bible speaks of women whom the ages ought to rise and call blessed. Think not, dear reader, that biblical records of human achievement look askance at the contributions of women in the centuries-long relation of God and his people. From Adam's day to the establishing of the Christian church the role of women was prominent and essential. Indeed, it is clear that without the part women played throughout those centuries the achievements of men would have been considerably less, or even nonexistent in some cases.

As the stories told in verse within this book attest, women were called on to make daring contributions, often risking their lives, that showed how far ahead of men they were in readiness to pray, to declare God's message to his and other people, to wait patiently on God, to sacrifice their most prized possessions (family, homeland) and to wage war when necessary. It is amazing to consider how many of Israel's greatest men were nurtured and directed at critical times by women. Thus, Sarah overruled her husband Abraham in the matter of Ishmael and the son was sent away; thus Abigail defied her husband's command and prepared food for David and his army when he was bent on destroying all her husband's men; thus Esther defied King Xerxes' command and approached the throne to plead, ultimately, that her people be spared; thus Mary Magdalene joined with other women, mostly poor, to minister to Jesus and his apostles "out of their own means;" and thus Priscilla, with her husband, welcomed the great Apollos into their home and "explained to him the way of God more adequately," while Lydia opened her home to homeless Paul and his friends.

These women did so much more than rock the cradle for they moved the hand of God. They addressed their men as "lord" but their wisdom and faith often far surpassed that of their men. Their prayers reached heaven long before men knew they needed to pray.

But let the stories speak for themselves; how a woman led the Israelite procession in praise while the bodies of Pharaohs' men were washing up on the Red Sea's eastern shore; how a woman sheltered two spies and assured Israel's first great victory in the Promised Land; how a woman prayed against heavy odds (her husband's disbelief and the priest's scornful rebuke) and gave to Israel its first and greatest prophet of the Kingdom era; how a woman went to battle when God's chosen man would not, and defeated a great Canaanite general; how a woman alone was singled out for giving her entire fortune (two coins) to the temple treasury; how a woman gave testimony and brought her townspeople to hear the words of Jesus; and how a woman disdained her obligations to guests and showed the true value of Jesus' teaching by sitting at his feet to learn.

These and other women bore testimony in quiet testing and joyous praise to God's goodness. Yes, kind reader, you will find a very different picture of women in these biblical accounts than what is commonly thought. I have put 45 of them into verse for your increased reading pleasure, especially if you will read them aloud for eye and ear to converse.

A Word about This Second Edition

I have written fifteen new poems on women in the Bible since first publishing Women of the Bible: Their Stories in Verse (c 2005). These poems include such key women as Leah, Rachel, Miriam and Queen Jezebel. They deserve a place in this new edition. Other women in the Bible, though barely mentioned or inferred such as Jephthah's daughter, Tamar, the Hebrew servant girl in General Naaman's home, and the wives of Samuel, Peter and Pilate, arouse intriguing interest as we speculate on their lives in the midst of powerful men and cultural forces that tended to disregard or deny any meaningful place for them in society. They have found their place in this book.

A second motive for re-publishing this book is to improve the meter and a few phrases in some lines in the first edition, remove some commas and clear up some of the typos which the first edition contained.

This edition also provides Biblical references that accompany each poem.

James Vasquez
February, 2009

Eve

(Gen. 3)

Midst rustling leaves of autumn hues
Reflecting as they fell
The sun's bright rays that pierced the woods,
Where bird and flower dwell,

I was escorted to his side,
Creation of his bone,
And from a rib was formed that he
No more would be alone.

And gurgling streams ran gently by
And grasses whispered low,
As cool and pleasant breezes did
Their fragrant scent bestow.

And waking from his sleep he held
My unrobed body near,
As if complete he sensed himself
And longed that I appear.

Now Adam was this man's good name,
First of his kind was he,
And Eve, a living mate for him
The name he gave to me.

The days we spent were filled and more
With joys on every side.

We thought their state would never change
But endless would abide.

For in our midst Another walked,
He called us day by day,
And in communion readily
We walked in all his way.

That fellowship so satisfied
All that within me dwelt,
And reached the limits of my soul
Which nothing lacking felt.

But in that place another walked,
Nay, let me say he crawled,
And by his suave, seductive charms
Deluded and enthralled.

But little did I know of this
Nor could I then have guessed,
I thought him but a creature like
Myself and all the rest!

And then one day he spoke to me,
Attentive, I gave ear,
So little thinking at the time
All that there was to fear.

And first he questioned whether I
Had not misunderstood
What God had said about the tree
Of evil and of good.

And then suggested there indeed
Was something that I lacked,

For eating of the tree I would
Be just like God in fact.

Still doubtful I then cast an eye
Upon that crimson fruit,
And how its loveliness appealed
I could not then dispute.

With hand outreached I grasped it and
Straight to my mouth in haste
I bore the succulent and knew
Its piquant, juicy taste.

And turning to dear Adam I
With hand held out once more
Then offered him the morsel too,
Nor needed to implore.

He took and then a silence reigned
Unlike all that I'd known,
And gone were all the rustling sounds
And songs of birds o'erflown.

The brook no longer babbled as
It made its rambling way,
And trees seemed strangely shorn of leaves,
Each branch in disarray.

The sky till then a sparkling blue
Was now foreboding red,
Though sunset still awaited us
And lay a while ahead.

And zephyrs carried not their scent
We were accustomed to,

And earth its freshness now had lost
From early morning dew.

And still another change there was
When Adam then revealed
A swatch of leaves insisting that
My body be concealed.

But yet the greatest change of all,
And one that caused us dread,
Was when we heard the voice of God
And from him quickly fled.

We'd heard him oft, his voice had been
A welcome, joyous thing,
But now it made our hearts to fear
And our base conscience sting.

We found ourselves a hiding place
Within a darkened glen,
But God once more called out to us
And Adam answered then.

And when God asked his whereabouts
He answered that he feared,
For lacking proper coverings
He naked thus appeared.

But little did these words deceive
Nor for a moment fool,
For God of Adam questioned well
About his foremost rule.

"And have you eaten of the tree
Of which I gave command,

Its fruit shall not pass through your lips
Nor feel your outstretched hand?"

Poor Adam now his fear increased,
Uncertain what to say.
With finger pointing straight at me,
He all but told God, "Nay!"

"The woman," he replied to God
Quite shaking in his fright,
"Was she who first consumed the fruit,
And then I took a bite."

"Please note," he might as well have said,
"The woman by my side
Is she whom you yourself produced
To live here and abide."

And turning then to me, God asked
That I an answer give,
And with no other folk around
I lacked alternative.

In truth I had but this to say,
"That slimy serpent there,
Spoke slyly of the things I lacked
Quite hoping to ensnare."

A curse God then invoked on him
And promised enmity,
For mortal consequences now
Our offspring were to see.

And mine would have his heel bruised,
And this unworthily,

But his a skull crushed underfoot
Would suffer fatally.

And with these words a hope remained
Though faint within our breast,
For in that sylvan circumstance
We failed to meet the test.

And then addressing me God said,
"Your pain will now increase,
In bringing forth each child henceforth,
And this without surcease.

"And for your husband," he then said,
"Shall your desire be,
Throughout your days you'll heed his voice
And follow his decree."

For Adam too God had these words,
"For you the ground is cursed,
And seeds of thistles and of thorns
Are everywhere dispersed.

"You listened to your wife and took
Its fruit from off the tree,
Now from your sweat and painful toil
Your days will not be free.

"Your years will not be endless but
A briefer, sad sojourn.
From dust you were created and
To dust you will return."

We left our home that saddened day,
In truth were driven out,

As cherubim stood guard with swords
That flamed and flashed about.

The memories I hold so dear
Of Adam and our days,
Together walking hand in hand
'Neath heaven's brilliant rays,

Bring sadness now as I reflect
On all that we have lost,
For that one simple trespass and
All that it finally cost.

But here's the thought I most review:
When Satan spoke that day,
My Adam was close by my side
And nothing did he say.

Cain's Wife

(Gen. 4)

Our lives are but a wandering,
We know not where each morn
Our weary feet will rest by night
When we are spent and worn.

The ground no longer yields its fruit
As in a long past year,
For only by Cain's labored brow
Might harvesting appear.

There was a time, he's said to me,
When thorns were quite unknown,
Nor was the ground then strewn with weeds
And goodly seeds were sown.

But things then took a fearful turn,
He would not tell me why.
And since that day life's been a curse
And will be till we die.

Yes life is hard, at times I think
'Tis more than I can bear,
And oft I've sought a friend with whom
My burdens I might share.

But Cain displays a mark so strange
Upon his flesh quite plain,

In fear all others soon withdraw
And friendship is in vain.

He told me of a brother who
Had disappeared one day.
The two were in a field and more
He simply would not say.

And closely then I questioned him
Just how the thing could be.
"Am I my brother's keeper?" was
His final word to me.

But of a past idyllic life
He frequently would speak.
His parents heard God's footsteps and
His presence then would seek.

"The place lies to the west," he said,
But would not tell me why
They left apace with heads bowed low
Beneath a threatening sky.

Nor would he lead me to the place
Nor scan it from afar.
"An angel stands with sword," he said,
"And does the pathway bar."

Now Cain's dear parents I know well,
They've lived in vilest grief,
As if some deed long past occurred
That gives them no relief.

Nor will they say what it might be
And yet some hope they've kept,

That one day things will turn around,
The things o'er which they've wept.

But Eve brought forth another son,
With Cain I happened by,
I heard the woman give the name
From midst a weary sigh.

She named him Seth: "For Abel whom
His brother meanly slew
Is now replaced within my home
And gladness reigns anew."

What horror then struck deep within!
What anguish filled my heart!
At last I understood just what
Had been my husband's part,

On that dark day when Abel was
No longer seen or heard,
For by the hand of Cain he fell
Without a further word.

And finally too, I understood
Just why the ground was cursed,
And why 'spite all Cain's ardent care
It ever was athirst.

I knew why there would be no place
That as a home we'd know,
But only far horizon's seek
And ever wandering go.

Now some have wondered whence I came,
It's yet to be explained,

But this I say assuredly,
'Twere better I remained.

Sarah—Mother of Nations
Wife of Abraham

(Gen. 12-23)

I called him master—so he was,
Who ruled by solemn word,
And quick was done the thing he asked,
Nor ever conflict heard.

'Cross many lands his fame was spread,
They at his name would bow.
And battles he had won afield
By sweat of furrowed brow.

A stranger when he first arrived,
He prospered greatly here,
As servants, cattle, horse and sheep
Were multiplied each year.

We wanted not possession or
Of comforts to delight,
For all our hearts could e'er desire
Was ours both day and night.

But greater satisfaction yet
Was ours when God inclined
To make a lasting pact with him
That would forever bind,

God's mercies to the needs of men
Where'er they might be found,

That through his servant Abraham
His kindness would abound.

Yes, kings would of his loins be born
And nations would be blessed,
And enmity 'tween God and men
Would know its final rest.

And I, God said, of nations would
A mother then become,
With progeny like stars above
So numberless in sum.

But now I tell you of the life
I lived from day to day,
For all is not as it appears
'Mongst those with feet of clay.

Now I was fair, they said of me
Of beauty quite endowed,
And with the passing of the years
My praise was sung aloud,

By men as everywhere I walked
My figure caught their eye,
But with my husband at my side,
Could nothing more than sigh.

And yet there was occasion when
My beauty was a peril,
'Mongst men who were of mightier sway
And anything but sterile.

Thus more than once he asked that I
His sister claim to be,

For fear his days would find their end
By those who longed for me.

But by God's favor it was learned
His wife I was instead,
Most fortunate for me before
They took me to the bed.

And I appreciated not
This manner that he showed.
I thought he was above such ways
And more to me he owed.

For as a man of faith he was
By then quite widely known.
At times I thought this property
Was somewhat overblown,

E'en though each time we prospered well
As on our way we went,
Enriched by those defrauded and
By them most duly sent.

But faults of mine were also seen
And now of them I speak,
For though I called him lord I was
At times not wholly meek.

I have in mind that you may hear
How barren I remained,
The promised child awaiting till
My faith was sadly strained.

And in an impulse one day said
That he should take my maid,

And by her then a child produce.
Well, he at once obeyed.

But troubles rose for when she found
A child she had conceived,
With spite she looked upon me and
Her loathing thus relieved.

In truth, confessing honestly,
I'll say my treatment of
This lass in kindness lacked a bit,
And even more in love.

She left one day, I'm confident
My anger drove her out.
Quite satisfied I was she'd left
Nor took the time to pout.

But God had other plans for her
And seldom he consults
His servants, less when they behave
Like petulant adults.

And so in God's good will once more
She took her place with us.
A friendlier home I vowed to have
Nor matters past discuss.

And Ishmael thus was born and placed
Upon my knees from birth,
In hopes his presence would suffice
To end our family dearth.

But such was not to be for God
Had promised us the heir

Would from our very loins be born,
Which I myself would bear.

I heard him from my tent one day
Addressing Abraham,
And hearing then I laughed and said,
"Old lady that I am?"

But nothing from God's ear is hid,
"And why did Sarah laugh?
Is this too great a thing," he asked,
"To do on your behalf?"

But I denied I laughed and this
He heard as well and said,
"Indeed, you laughed." And I was left
Well flushed of face and red.

And nothing more was needed by
That eager man of mine,
Not coaxing or coquettish form
Nor goblets filled with wine.

And need I say within a year
Just as God said 'twould be,
Upon a night of suffering long
A son was born to me.

We named him Isaac for it seemed
Our sorrow he replaced.
We laughed at all adversity
Together we had faced.

And shortly there were problems as
The son my servant bore

I saw in mocking tone address
My Isaac and I swore,

That Ishmael would not have a share
In Isaac's legacy,
And this to Abraham I said
As with divine decree.

And God confirmed this word to him
That he my word should heed,
And vowed to make of Ishmael
A mighty tribe indeed.

Our son was then brought up in peace,
Our home a sheltered place,
And daily then I yearned to see
The promised, holy race.

And yet our son has yet to find
A woman for his wife,
Through whom our progeny will know
An oath-appointed life.

But this, I fear, I now must leave
In Abra'am's worthy hands,
To search 'mongst Canaan's peoples or
In distant, foreign lands.

The years have known a fullness which
My God has greatly blessed.
And shortly when my life expires
My days shall find their rest.

Hagar—"The God Who Sees Me"

Sarah's maid - she was bought from Egypt - a slave
mother of Ishmael
Abraham's concubine
(Gen. 16, 21)

You've kindly come, dear friend, this hour
To spend most quietly with me,
As in my home we savor now
Quite freshly brewed Egyptian tea!

No matter if for years on end
I ate and drank what others had
In far off Canaan where as maid
My foreign customs they forbad.

A wealthy, elder couple they
Were hoping that a child be born,
Though quite beyond the years for this
And yet convinced that God had sworn,

Avowing that despite their age
The wife in time a son would bear,
Who would be their delight each day
And of their great possessions heir.

So if with cup in hand just now
You're ready to give ear to me,
I'll tell my tale. (The tea is good!
Refreshing well, do you agree?)

I served them faithfully each day,
Their language and their customs learned,

32

Was diligent in all I did
And favor with them both I earned.

I deeply felt for Sarah who
In spite of effort and of will
Could not conceive that male child
Who finally would the vow fulfill.

Now things went well I say until
My masters seemed to give up hope.
But life without a son was not
A thing with which they wished to cope.

Their eyes then fell on me one day
As if this maid could be the source
From which their longed-for son would come.
(Another cup of tea? Of course!)

So Abraham consented to
His wife's sweet gift – of me, no less!
He took me for a wife in hopes
That God our union would then bless.

Now I was young, no lines had left
Those tell-tale marks of age on me,
And pretty, with Egyptian charm
As Pharoahs wished their wives to be.

And so with Abraham I learned
Before the dawn's first welcome light,
How greatly he desired a son
And slept but little through the night.

Now you will understand, dear friend,
With opportunities galore,

I surely would conceive, e'en fate
Cannot man's penchants long ignore.

O'er time I started to dislike
And then my mistress to abhor.
I knew the child would not be mine,
For her my miseries I bore.

She spoke to Abraham and said
The blame was his for what occurred,
And then so harshly treated me
By hostile deed and spiteful word,

I fled and found a lonely place
Beside a desert spring where I
Beneath a warming sun could rest,
Where I some peace would find - and die.

'Twas there an angel sought me out,
An angel sent from God above.
'Twas there I first began to know
That even me this God could love.

He asked me whence I came and where
I thought to go and then I said
I knew not whither I would go
But that from Sarah I had fled.

He spoke again and for his words
My life has never been the same.
Once more I felt there was a God
Who sees me in the depths of shame.

He promised my descendants would
Be many and hold mighty sway,

That I would bear a son whose name
Of Ishmael would be great one day.

Yet he would be, the angel said,
A wild donkey of a man,
His hand against all others and
Adversely living midst his clan.

But I was to return, he said,
For God's good plan to realize,
Submitting to my mistress nor
To disobey or compromise.

And then I knew that I had seen
The One who sees me in my need.
I felt his presence, heard his voice
And had no wish but to accede. *agree*

The day arrived and Ishmael
Upon my mistress' lap was born.
She took the child as if her own,
No longer saddened or forlorn.

The years passed quickly and one day
To father Abraham's surprise,
My mistress whispered in his ear
A thing that opened wide his eyes.

She was with child she proudly said
And Abraham, a hundred now,
Throughout the camp ran quickly or,
As legs that ancient would allow,

To spread the word that all might know
God's promise would be soon fulfilled.

A son from Sarah's womb would come,
The very thing they both had willed.

I pondered then just what this meant
For I received a promise, too.
Had he who sees me turned aside?
Would I God's kindly words now rue?

But few years thence the child was weaned
And Ishmael in playful tone,
Repeated words the child had said
In baby talk as all were prone.

Well, what a fuss old Sarah raised!
Perhaps because of every guest
Invited on that special day
When kids are taken off the breast.

To Abraham she said aloud,
(The guests had hardly left the door!),
"Now rid this house of Hagar and
The son upon my lap she bore!

"He'll not inherit with my son
The promises God gave to us!"
And Abraham, distressed because
His wife had raised this strident fuss,

About his son whom he had loved,
Found prayer in solitude anew.
And then he heard the voice of God
Instructing him in what to do.

"Be not distressed, my Abraham,
Nor Ishmael's destiny bemoan.

Heed all that Sarah says to you,
Through Isaac will your seed be known.

"And I will make of Ishmael
A nation strong upon the earth,
And care as well for Hagar who
Brought him to light and gave him birth."

And so it was, by sun's first rays
Of dawn next day we both were sent
With food and water on our backs,
But lacking beast to help and tent.

Dismissed by Abraham this way
We wandered in the desert till
With water gone, 'neath blazing sun,
I finally had no strength or will.

I put the boy beneath a bush
And wandered off a ways to cry.
'Twas then I heard the voice once more
Of him who sees me with his eye.

From heav'n it came and said to me,
"What troubles you? Be not afraid.
For God the cries of Ishmael hears
From where you hid him in the shade.

"Now lift the boy and by the hand
Lead him to meet his destined fate,
For I have vowed of him to make
A mighty nation vast and great."

My eyes were fully opened then,
By God who truly all things sees.

A well of water there appeared
In answer to my fervent pleas.

(You think you'd like another cup?
Just let me stoke the fire once more.
Egyptian tea is best when hot,
In but a moment then, I'll pour.)

Now God was with my son as vowed.
In Paran's desert, tall and strong,
An expert archer he became
And still they tell of him in song.

And one more thing I did for him
Ere we could prosper or survive,
A wife from Egypt I secured
That he might keep our ways alive.

Rebekah

(Gen. 22-29)

[handwritten annotation: Wife of Issac]

[handwritten annotation: Issac prayed for her to have a child — she had twins. Jacob/Esau]

My name was known among our clan
Of eastern peoples where
No talk by men exceeded that
Of unwed virgins fair.

And though quite young it yet was clear
My features did display
With just a glance from top to toe
What had been mere hearsay.

Now such was I within my tent
Where serving well each day,
My duties I attended and
Alone each night I lay.

For father had not yet observed
The man he worthy thought
To claim me as his own, indeed,
He quite disdained the lot.

Or if one ventured to our door
And prospects thus renewed,
"Twas found his purse was void as ours
Which father's hopes subdued.

And I was not displeased in truth,
For I'd not met the man

'Mongst suitors who within my soul
A passioned love could fan,

Since I an emptiness had known
Midst many a prayer and sigh,
An emptiness within my soul
That naught could satisfy,

Though I had learned a man of faith
Once lived within our race,
But when a call from God was heard
He left without a trace.

And oh! If fate would grant that I
But once with him might walk,
I'd learn if life was more than but
Four walls, a meal and talk.

Yes, ease of life which many sought
Was mine I'd say and yet,
It scarcely brought me happiness
Nor deeper longings met.

Would I at last pursue in vain
My soul's tranquility?
Would God direct his watchful eye
My pitied life to see?

I knew not how to answer but
These searchings then set fire
Each day more ardently to all
I willed or could desire.

Well on a recent day as I
My daily chores observed,

There came a man who all my hopes
Quite wonderfully preserved.

He asked if from my water jar
I might relieve his thirst,
His camels too I watered then
Though we had not conversed.

He watched as if in deepest thought
Each movement that I made,
As quickly I performed the task,
Nor tired nor delayed.

And to my great surprise he drew
From treasures he had stored
A gift or two of gold for me,
And kindly then implored,

That I my father's name reveal
In hopes he'd find a place
Where he might lodge and rest his beasts,
Perhaps a meal embrace.

I knew him not but sensed a man
Of privilege he was,
And welcomed him to find his rest,
As every maiden does.

But not before I told him of
The lineage that was mine,
The name of each within our tent
When with us he would dine.

And bowing then, he uttered praise
Most heart-felt from within,

And thanked the Lord for leading him
To his dear master's kin!

Now Abraham was he who sent
This servant on his way,
And when he uttered that good name
As he went on to pray,

I hardly could contain myself
For much I'd heard of him,
And he it was who walked with God
In years long past and dim.

And could it be, I wondered then
But feared to ask aloud,
God heard my prayer and through this man
On bended knee and bowed,

Would satisfy the deepest part
Of my soul's long pursuit,
And banishing its emptiness
My aching void dispute?

And straight to family I repaired
To tell of what I'd learned,
But ere my brother heard the half,
Within a craving burned.

For when he saw adorning me
The gifts of gold I wore,
He hurried out to meet the man
His presence to implore.

"Now come, O blessed of the Lord,
A place is well prepared,

For you, your men and all your beasts,"
He hopefully declared.

And food was placed before the man
But ere he would partake,
His story he had need to tell,
His promise not to break.

"I prayed to God that one would come,
A daughter strong and fair,
And waited close beside the well
In hopes I'd find her there.

"And she of whom I begged a drink
Who then replied to me,
She'd water all my camels, would
God's chosen maiden be.

"For I have come from far away
A proper wife to seek,
O'er foreign lands and wind-blown trails
And scorching deserts bleak,

"To find among my master's kin
The one his son might wed,
And finally by God's mighty hand
To this dear lass I'm led.

"And if your hearts are so inclined
Such kindness now to show,
Please tell me or if not then I
Another path will know."

And quite amazed my father was,
With brother Laban too.

"The thing is of the Lord," they said,
"And what are we to do?"

And I attended well his words
And all he had to say,
Of how he prayed and God had heard
And led him on the way.

Within my heart I strongly sensed
That emptiness so vast,
Would finally know its end as I
This God embraced at last.

So when they asked if I would go
Or further celebrate,
Quite ready to depart was I
And know my chosen fate.

Then costly gifts this servant gave,
Of clothing, silver, gold,
And if my loss a sadness brought
My family was consoled.

A blessing they bestowed that all
My offspring might increase,
And at the gate of enemies
Prevail in lasting peace.

Our journey now has found its end,
Their tents afar I see,
And lo! A man within a field
Who now approaches me.

The servant tells me this is he,
His master's favored son,

The heir of all his master's wealth
For whom his search was done.

A look of peace I then behold,
Of contemplative mien,
And closer now it seems there is
A smile of kindness seen.

Alighting then, with face well veiled
I wait to take his hand,
And sense the reason for my trials
I finally understand.

Leah

(Gen. 29-35, 49)

A mother to my people's clan
    Would all my destiny fulfill,
For half of Israel's tribes were born
Of my rich womb and God's good will.

But lest you think, my friend, that life
    Held nothing less for me in store
Than honor and high privilege, hear,
    As I recount those days of yore.

I suffered much though secretly
    For reasons that I now explain,
And wish that you might understand
    But from all pity please refrain.

For though my tale of sadness speaks,
    'Tis but that you might know it best,
And since at last God evens things,
    I am 'mongst women truly blest.

I did not always see things thus
    For early was I made aware
My sister, younger by a year,
    Was lovelier of form and fair.

Yes such the beauty of her face
    At once she caught the eye of men,

46

Handwritten margin notes:

unloved wife of
Jacob, 1st wife
Older sister of Jacob's
second wife, Rachel.
mother of Jacob's first
son, Reuben.
mother of Simeon,
Levi, Judah,
Issachar,
Zebulun, &
Dinah.

Jacob loved
Rachel who
did not have
children.

Jacob

Israel

A quick "hello" to me if that,
And at her feet they tumbled then.

And so one day a man came by,
A wanderer from some far off land.
He was our kin and stayed to work,
And did whatever was at hand.

But thirty days had hardly passed
And he was smitten to the gills,
In such a way, 'twas plain to see,
That only death or marriage stills.

He pleaded for her hand at once
And father, bless his soul, agreed.
He'd work sev'n years to claim his wife,
But this was quite against our creed.

For I as older sister must
By right be giv'n in marriage first,
And knowing this our father then,
This simple plan with me rehearsed.

When darkness filled the tent by night
He led me, not my sister, there,
And Jacob's yearning, oh! 'twas such
Not once all night was he aware!

And so we spent the night and bliss
Once longed for then was fully mine,
Alas! Till dawn's first light broke forth
And rid us of the night and wine.

"What wanton trickery is this?!"
He snorted loudly as he rose,

And straight to father made his way
His uncurbed anger to disclose.

(Had he so soon forgot those hours
So filled with pleasures and delight,
And amorous words beyond all count
That he had whispered through the night?)

'Twas then he learned just how our ways
So different from his own were done,
And Rachel would be his at last
For sev'n more years beneath the sun.

Now wives were meant to bear fine sons
As every father knew so well,
And pity then, the woman who
Of no such progeny could tell.

And here another wrong I knew
For when a son I brought to life,
I thought his love I'd surely gain
And find contentment as his wife.

'Twas not to be I sensed at once,
And though another son I bore,
My hopes remained quite unfulfilled,
He loved but Rachel more and more.

A third I bore and thought at least
Some sweet attachment now for sure
Within my husband should awake
That would my hopes once more bestir.

A forth I bore and saw no change,
He loved but Rachel come what may,

Rachel

Though God had closed her womb and naught
From her came forth to light of day.

Now what remained for me to do?
In desperation then my maid
I offered that by her at last,
His longed-for love I might persuade.

She bore him two and then I thought
Good fortune had arrived for me,
And happy, every woman said,
My striving life had come to be.

It finally came to this, my friend,
Nor love nor sweet attachment grew.
By day he spoke no tender word
Nor e'er by night his touch I knew.

You think the worst had come? I ask,
Now listen and be entertained,
For I will tell you plainly how
His "services" once more I gained.

It happened thus: fair Rachel asked
That I some plant would share with her.
I thought her brash for this request
And with her plea did not concur.

"My husband you have taken and
These plants you'd have as well?" I said.
"Then in return," she said, "this night
He'll sleep within your tent instead."

I felt I'd reached the lowest point
But shared with Jacob when he came

Just how I'd bought him for the night,
With little hesitance or shame.

Nor was he shamed to join me then,
For Rachel had this tryst allowed,
And once again my prayer was heard
For God another son avowed.

No change I saw in Jacob yet
And so another son I bore.
He was the sixth (and last!) I had,
Enough I thought to grace our lore.

Leah

I'd sought his love and found it not,
Some close attachment but fell short,
Would he at least now honor me
And thus display some small support?

You'll know, kind friend, when you have done
With this my tale so plainly told.
Now hear as I relate at last
A final wrong I knew of old.

LABAN
Leah & Rachel's
father

For as the years their journey made
We sensed in father's love some change.
He looked upon his daughters more
As foreigners and somewhat strange.

He cancelled our inheritance
And wasted all the wealth he gained,
As Jacob worked his fields for years,
Nor weariness nor sickness feigned.

And thus when Jacob summoned us
With all our children that last day,

To leave our father's house with him
And journey south without delay,

We found ourselves quite in accord
For God had called him to return
To Canaan's land whence he had come,
A lasting blessing there to earn.

We saw our father yet again
When he o'er took us on a hill,
But he had been forewarned of God
To speak no word of good or ill.

We celebrated long that night
And bid goodbye as families can,
And early left for that far land
Where Jacob's story first began.

And here my story finds its end.
There's not much more that speaks of me
Within our lore for 'tis my sons
Who from this time made history.

*****

In this was Leah's honor found,
'Twas she not Rachel laid to rest
Within the cave with Abraham
At Jacob's very own request.

Rachel

I well remember that warm day
When first I saw him yet ahead,
A stranger as my sheep I coaxed
And to the covered well I led.

And as the stone set on the well
He moved in kindness and alone,
No thought had I of who he was
And little of him could have known.

But in these lingering moments now,
Unsure what will become of me,
My thoughts I fix on all he did
And how things finally came to be.

A stranger yes, but also kin
And soon I learned the stranger's name.
'Twas Jacob and the sight of me
At once set all his heart aflame.

Of form and face most lovely I
Was shepherdess to father's sheep,
And longed instead of animals
A man and joyful home to keep.

He met my father and a month
Had scarcely passed when he proposed.

He'd work sev'n years to gain my hand,
And thus his ardent love disclosed.

For much he favored me but not
My sister Leah, dim of sight,
Though custom urged the elder first
Be duly wed to make things right.

He worked and how he prospered then!
Or should I say, my father did.
The wealth he gained was seen by all
Nor from our watchful vision hid.

Now did I say sev'n years? In truth,
They seemed much quicker to expire,
No doubt for all the thought he gave
To me and his intense desire.

The night thus came, a gala feast
My father held with much to drink.
And Jacob in the darkened tent
Performed his right nor paused to think,

Till morning when by dawn's first light
He saw 'twas Leah by his side.
My father had ordained it so
That Jacob by our rules abide.

To say the least he was surprised
But quite becalmed when father said
That for another seven years,
I would be his to love and bed.

Now oft I've wondered how it was
He passed the night with Leah there,

But thought throughout that it was I,
While of the facts quite unaware.

And so within the week we wed
And he at once his work began,
But if he thought he'd entered heav'n
Surprises yet besieged the man.

His wages father often changed
Though not in keeping with his work,
For Jacob brought prosperity
Nor from a hardship would he shirk.

But if outside the home there were
Such problems as he had not known,
Within the discord was far worse
That daily he was forced to own.

The problem, you will understand,
Was simply that while Leah gained
Much favor by the sons she bore
—I was quite barren and complained.

Indeed she bore four sons and then
Her maid as well delivered two.
My maid I offered then and soon
Yet two more sons made their debut.

"Now give me children or I die!"
I told my husband to persuade.
"And am I God," he answered me,
"Who has your womb so barren made?"

But he who hears our every plea
Aroused himself to answer then,

54

I was with child and Jacob learned
And was the happiest of men.

Well things went worse out in the field
For Jacob by our father's hand.
About that time God said to him,
"Return now to your native land."

And when he told us of his plan
We were at once quite in accord,
For father thought us foreigners,
From him we looked for no reward.

We left by stealth one early morn
When father was away with sheep.
We took our many things and I
Our household idols wished to keep.

But then in Gilead he came,
My father with an angry throng,
Full bent on doing us willful harm
Nor ruing that it might be wrong.

But this amazing tale he told,
The Lord appeared to him and said
That neither good or bad was he
To say to Jacob who had fled.

"But why have you not granted me
To kiss my daughters a goodbye?
Nor yet their children to embrace,
Perhaps to shed a tear and cry?

"A feast I would have held at once
And honored you with music sweet,

Dismissing with my blessing and
A joyful sendoff as is meet."

He did of course make mention of
The idols I had filched and hid,
But searching he uncovered naught
As I their whereabouts bestrid. *straddle*

"The way of women has now come,"
I said remaining on the ground,
(The idols 'neath my outspread skirt),
Which turned my father quite around.

Cause to become muddled or obscure.

Now once again uncertainty
Beclouds my mind as pains increase,
But I must yet conclude my tale,
Make haste my soul, and be at peace.

'Twas quite a scene we witnessed there
As Laban and my Jacob met,
But in the end accord was reached
Without undue constraint or threat.

A heap of stones, a pillar too,
They set between themselves that day.
And taking oath they promised each
For harm they'd never cross that way.

And sorrowing for his daughters and
Their children whom he'd never see,
My father said, "Now God is judge,
A witness e'er 'tween you and me."

We parted then, but not without
A feast in honor of the day,

And in the morn midst hugs and tears
Our last respects we each did pay.

My time grows short, I hasten now,
Yet one last memory remains.
I'll tell you briefly how it came
Midst bitter suffering and pains.

My husband long had feared the day
When Esau would his presence find,
For he had wronged this brother once
And knew that vengeance filled his mind.

He came upon us shortly then,
And with an army at his side,
Our hearts were filled with fear, we had
No place to run or even hide.

But once again the ways of God
Turned all our thinking quite around.
He greeted Jacob kindly and
As if some long-lost brother found.

And how I wish this babe within
My body now would come to light!
My strength is waning fast I feel,
While here I labor through the night.

And will they treat my Joseph well
When I'm no longer by his side?
And will his brothers show him love
And some encouragement provide?

Or will his father's favor be
Sufficient to their ways amend?

I know not but with final breath
My soul I now to God commend.

Death of Rachel

Israel's Song

(Ex. 15)

Song of Moses and Miriam

Ex. 15:21 Miriam sings -

Sing loud your tributes, Israel,
Let not your tongue be dumb,
Nor silent now your heart's acclaim
Whence all your praises come.

This poem refers to when God opened the Red Sea so the Israelites could pass through.

And fill the air with songs of joy,
Exalt the name on high
Of God who reigns majestically
O'er earth and sea and sky.

For none there was to hear the call,
Their desperate, futile plea,
As horse and rider by his might
Were cast into the sea.

Pharoah's horsemen were swallowed by the sea.

And Pharoah's army was destroyed
Pursuing Israel's clan.
The waters closed upon the host
And left there not a man.

Now my salvation he will be,
This God of war and song,
My father's God exalted high,
For whom my praises long.

The captains in distress cried out
And those of highest rank,

But none rose up to rescue them
And like a stone they sank.

O Israel now sing to God
And raise your voice this hour,
Today your very ears have heard,
Your eyes beheld his power.

And Pharoah knew your servant's voice
But scoffed at your command.
His army thus was shattered by
The strength of your right hand.

Your anger burned and when unleashed
The enemy consumed,
As surging waters covered them
Who in their depths were doomed.

For they had boasted of the spoils
In words of lofty pride,
Allotting each a share in what
They'd have by eventide.

But when a single breath from you
Brought down the crested sea,
Like lead they plunged beneath the waves,
Which vanquished every plea.

Now lift your voice to God above
And sing rejoicingly,
Give thanks to him, O Israel,
For this great victory.

For with a mighty hand outstretched
His awesome power to show,

He split the earth, its cleavage yawned
And swallowed up the foe.

The kings of Edom are dismayed,
In Moab will they quake,
The citizens of Canaan bow,
Their leave will fondly take.

And silent as a stone are they
For dread upon them fell.
They know 'tis God who goes before
The tribe of Israel.

Our people pass them by unharmed,
They dare not lift a hand.
In vain they think to turn aside
Our march to promised land.

And Miriam the prophetess
With ringing tambourine,
Then danced before the people with
A joyful, stately mien.

And joined at once in song by all
The women in her train,
Went forth throughout our joyous tribes
And chanted this refrain,

Adore your God, O Israel,
And sing his majesties,
Who stands alone in terrible deeds
Above all deities.

Now let your mouths his glories sing,
To him your praises be,

For horse and rider of the foe
Were hurled into the sea.

Miriam

Moses' sister
Moses married a Cushite

(Ex. 15; Num. 12)

A basket made of reeds afloat
Upon the Nile serenely set,
Was I to watch, to see perchance
What fate or accident it met.

And wrapped within, secure against
The cold of early morning dew,
My brother with his infant cries
Was softly heard though out of view.

For not yet weaned he longed to know
The tender breast that life supplied,
As babes but three months old will do
Before they slumber, satisfied.

Now Pharoah ordered all midwives
Each newborn Hebrew son to slay.
But mother much preferred to leave
Her infant as a castaway.

And shortly then, good fortune brought
A woman with her maidens fair,
Who heard the babe's determined cries
And quickly was inclined to care.

To bathe she'd come but then instead,
She sent to fetch him from his plight,

And viewing there his lovely face
Was filled that moment with delight.

She took him in her arms and quick
Was I to make my presence known.
And then I saw the amulets,
The rings and bracelets she did own.

For gold adorned her head to toe,
And who she was at once I knew,
'Twas Pharoah's daughter who had come
Surrounded by her retinue.

Now I was but a girl myself,
Of humble origin and clan,
And bowing then respectfully,
And somewhat shyly as girls can,

I asked if she might wish that I
Some woman seek to nurse the child,
Until once weaned and on that day
He'd be returned. And then she smiled.

"Well thought, my child," the princess said,
"And for such service I will pay.
Now haste and search most carefully.
Look hither, yon without delay."

I searched not long, I knew of course
Jut where the woman would be found.
And so to home I scurried with
This news to make her joy abound.

My mother raised her son three years
And then to Pharoah's house she went,

Whose daughter named him Moses for
"From waters of the Nile he's lent."

Now these but early memories were.
There's yet more that I have to tell
Of Moses, brother, royal prince,
In Egypt's ways instructed well.

A favorite then, in Pharoah's house
And destined for some greater fame,
But when he killed a man he thence
Would live within the land in shame.

He fled and for some forty years
We knew not where or yet with whom,
And little did we think that God
Had borne him yon to teach and groom.

And then one day quite suddenly
A man in shepherd's dress appeared,
His eyes ablaze with untamed zeal,
'Twas Moses, gaunt and desert-seared.

We heard how God was sending him,
My brother Moses to break loose
The chains that had enslaved us all
And end our shameful, sad abuse.

The wonders then, that he performed!
All Egypt soon lay at his feet,
And with the death of first-born sons
The nation's ruin was complete!

A way within the sea was made
And safely were we led within

Until we reached the distant shore,
Each weary family and its kin.

But Pharoah's army pressing hard
To overtake us in the way
Was swallowed up, a vengeful sea
Cared not to hear them cry or pray.

For Moses had stretched forth his arm
Commanding thereby that the sea
Envelop horse and rider, thus
Each met his end by God's decree.

But lest I bore you with his tale
I'll turn my thoughts most modestly
To my peculiar role that day
In Israel's victory by the sea.

For with a tambourine in hand
I led the way in dance and song,
While women followed in my train,
In skimpy blouse and gay sarong.

A song of praise we lifted then
To God the Lord, exalted high,
Who overcame a host of men
Trained well to kill and drawing nigh.

Now if my story full and true
I am to tell you, hear me now.
There came a day much to my shame
I can't deny or disavow,

When with my brother Aaron I
Rose up against authority.

"Did not the Lord as well through us
Give promise of our legacy?"

'Gainst Moses did we speak that day
For we were bothered by his wife,
A Cushite she, though never known
To stir the pot or create strife.

Then called before the Lord we knew
How great our sin and our disgrace,
For God put us in mind of how
He spoke to Moses face to face.

In anger then he left us and
The cloud departed high above.
I stood in fear and wonder there,
My skin as white as any dove.

But Aaron pleaded for me well.
"Oh! let this leprosy depart!
Hold not this sin against us and
Some mercy, brother, now impart."

So Moses prayed most earnestly,
"My sister, Lord, please deign to heal.
Let not this punishment endure,
Once more your charity reveal."

And I for sev'n days was without
The camp, a penalty to pay,
According to our Law's demand
For those who willf'ly disobey.

And here I close my lengthy tale,
You've lent your ear most graciously.

May God be praised, redeeming us
From bondage he has set us free.

Ráhab—The Fall of Jerico

prostitute

Rahab & the spies

(Jos. 2, 6; Heb. 11; Jas. 2) *Faith in Action*

Heb. 11:31

My name brought twisted smiles from men
And commonly was slurred
In Jerico or fields around,
Wherever it was heard.

Yes I was known both here and yon
For hospitality,
But of a kind, I will confess,
That brought ill fame to me.

I know not how it was that I
A harlot came to be,
But those who most reproved my ways
Were those who called on me.

For I was loved by many men *prostitute*
But always would I know
Outside my home they'd look away
And never kindness show.

My home was in a mighty wall,
Each day guests came and went,
But living thus could not fulfill,
An emptiness it lent.

There came one eve two foreign men
Soon after I had dined

Who sought from me a courtesy
But of a different kind.

They asked that I might hide them and
Say nothing of their stay,
And spoke in no uncertain terms
Of an approaching day,

When with an army they would come
And sweep across our land,
Destroying towns and people and
Allowing none to stand.

Now we had heard an army was
Approaching Jordan's banks,
With little thought of mercy or
Of peace within its ranks.

And also then, I heard as well
They claimed as their true God
The One who all the heavens made,
And earth where man had trod.

And he in holiness had led
His armies in the fight,
And such his strength his enemies
Were slaughtered in their flight.

Our hearts then melted out of fear,
No people had withstood
This wasting army of the Lord,
And none we reckoned could.

Our city stood within their path
As ruthless they marched on.

And thus a notion came to mind
Which I then seized upon.

I'd hide them well as they had asked
If they in turn would swear
The day they marched on us to fight
My family's life to spare.

And this included mine of course,
Along with all my kin,
Whom I would gather in my home
To shelter them within.

"Agreed," they said, and to the roof
I led them quickly then.
I knew the king would send in search
Of these mysterious men.

I hid them thus 'neath stocks of flax
That I was drying there,
And told the soldiers they had come
But then had gone elsewhere.

"But hurry now, they've not gone far,
They left at close of day.
You'll surely catch them," I declared,
"If you'll be on your way."

The soldiers left and ere I laid
My head upon the bed
I spoke again to my two guests,
Confirming all we said.

"Our lives for yours," they then assured,
"For with a kindly hand

We'll deal with you and all your kin
When God gives us this land."

And as a sign they gave to me
A lengthy, scarlet cord,
Which hanging from my window would
Our safety thus afford.

For Israel's soldiers would then know
That here their men had found
A refuge and a place to rest
While treading foreign ground.

And late that night I lowered them
From out my window there,
And sent them to the hills awhile,
This furtive, spying pair.

And thus it happened one day soon
An army had appeared,
Across the distant, sun-baked plain,
And slowly then, it neared,

Until around our city's wall
It camped forebodingly,
A vast, victorious host of men
Encircling like the sea.

And need I say how fear then struck
The boldest heart around,
As we beheld the Lord's army
And heard the trumpets sound?

For daily would they march outside
Our stout and lofty wall,

As if expecting that somehow
It could be made to fall,

While priests behind the soldiers marched
With trumpets well in hand,
And blew their loudest as they strode
As if at God's command.

And early on the seventh day
They rose to march again,
And marched around full seven times,
These bold, determined men.

"Now shout," their leader ordered them
As trumpets finally blew,
"Today this mighty Jerico,
Our God has given you!"

And then so unexpectedly,
A loud and dreadful sound
Throughout our city and beyond
Did everywhere resound.

And nothing less it was than this,
Our sturdy, lofty wall
By some great force came crashing down
And 'neath it, crushing all.

And then two men outside my door
Commanded that we leave.
It was the men I sheltered who
Would now their debt relieve.

And thus while Israel's army fought
With sword and shield and spear,

Destroying all of Jerico,
Its people far and near,

I with my family was kept safe
And from a distant post,
Observed the wretched slaughter of
This city and its host.

I heard their leader Joshua
Proclaim in strident voice
That whoso would rebuild the place
Would make a fateful choice,

For at the cost of his firstborn
Foundations would he lay,
And e'en the youngest born to him
His life would he betray.

Now time has passed and thought I've giv'n
To each grim memory,
Just how it happened as it did
And why it had to be.

My early years I knew not God
And I revered him not.
Midst Israel's throng I've found that he
Is what I'd always sought.

For even an avenging God
Will look upon and scan
Each proud and vile activity
Of woman and of man.

And to those who most ready seem
To turn from lives of sin,

He offers them a helping hand,
A new life to begin.

And when I seek to understand
The turn my life would take,
"The fall of Jerico," I say,
"He did it for my sake."

Deborah—March on, My Soul

prophetess

*Judges 4:4 Deborah was
judging Israel* (Jud. 4, 5)
at this time.

*Judges 4:6
mt. Tabor*

I will sing to the Lord a song
Of triumph o'er the foe,
The Canaanite army subdued
And Sisera brought low.

The stars in their courses looked on
And from the heavens fought
'Gainst Sisera's army deployed,
And of his host made naught.

The earth convulsed, the heavens poured,
The clouds their waters gushed.
Great Sinai's God once more appeared,
And battle cries were hushed.

The horses' hooves then thundered loud
As galloping away
They left their riders bloodied, still,
Forsaken where they lay.

Awake, O Deborah, and sing,
And music offer up,
Your vows of thanks are fitting now
Before this night you sup.

For Kishon's waters swept away
The last of Canaan's throng

That twenty years oppressed our land.
March on, my soul, be strong!

But quiet were the village streets
As waiting distant knell,
Until I rose a mother to
My cherished Israel.

And prophetess was I before
The Lord who had ordained
That I should judge my people while
Their fortunes sadly waned.

But when they cried to God for help
With honest, fervent plea,
His tender ear was open for
He rose to set us free.

Then calling out from Zebulun
And also Naphtali,
Ten thousand men most brave I chose
Who weren't afraid to die.

And when my own commander said
He'd fight if I would go,
I went and said the glory then,
A woman was to know.

"Go forth! This day the Lord has giv'n
Into your hand," I said,
"This host whose men by evening sun
Will fall before you dead."

And princes from yon Issachar,
And Ephraim's stalwart young,

And valiant men from Benjamin
To battle quickly sprung.

Be strong my soul to praise such men
Who willingly arose,
Though lacking sword and spear with which
An army to oppose.

But God led forth the march they took,
The Canaanite was slain,
Save Sisera who fled on foot
Across the scarlet plain.

Now Jael, keeper of a tent,
Received this beaten man,
And thus became the woman who
Would satisfy God's plan.

She gave him milk, she gave him rest,
She covered him in sleep.
And through his wearied temple then,
She drove a tent peg deep.

And Deborah's army in pursuit
Arrived in time to see
The fallen captain at her feet,
And Jael's victory!

But Reuben searches heart and soul,
He chose to stay behind
Midst campfires burning bright and warm,
With pleasures there to find.

And far beyond swift Jordan's flow
The men of Gilead

Were well apprised of Israel's need,
But sent not thence a lad.

While by the ships in waters calm
Dan's men of war still wait.
Now cursed be all who lingered thus,
And wretched be their fate.

And through a window peering out
A mother wonders long
Just why her son does not appear,
And asks what could be wrong.

"Tis surely that his chariot,"
Her maidens answer her,
"Is laden well with plundered gifts
You shortly will prefer."

So may your enemies expire
As Sisera this day,
But those who love you, Lord, will shine
As does the sun's bright ray.

a mighty warrior

Jephthah's Daughter

only child

Jephthah made a vow
to the Lord if the Lord
would help him in a (Jud. 11)
Battle, when he got Judges 11:29-40
home whoever meets
him at the door
he would
sacri'fice (kill)
to the Lord,
His daughter
was sacrificed,

I wanted naught for brother or
For sister yet to fill our home.
'Twas all I cared when father came,
And ceased some far off land to roam.

I lived alone with father and
In truth we had no further need,
Nor felt we lacked of anything
That we might ever wish or heed.

We had each other, God had willed
A father with his daughter thus.
happy home Our home was known for glad accord
And many surely envied us.

Commander of a host of men,
He'd gone the Ammonites to fight,
While I awaited hopefully,
For his appearance day and night.

And oft I'd flung myself at him
To greet him, joyful and with tears,
Nor can one know the grave concern
His absence caused me or the fears.

Then word arrived, he'd come at last!
I quickly readied self and place,

And when I heard the hoof beats stop
I longed to be in his embrace.

With ringing tambourine and clap
Of castanet I danced my way,
To him who came, a victor sure,
All my respects to warmly pay.

*DAncing +
Sound of
timBrels
⇓
tambourine*

But then the look I saw upon
His pallid face, within his eyes,
Bespoke a sense of horror he knew
That understanding e'er defies.

He screamed a scream I'd never heard,
My name he cried to heaven high.
Some thing or person brought his pain
And soon I learned that it was I. —

*she's
sAcrificed
to the
Lord.*

*****

Sweet maidens come, join with me now
A rose's fragrance to inhale.
This lasting mem'ry let me take
That our good friendship might prevail.

Mourn quietly, my friends, your loss,
That on this day we yet may know
Some pleasure or peculiar grace
A smiling fortune may bestow.

Now lightly tread this upward path
That we may look afar from high,
And scan soft fields where once we played,
Where soon my body, still, shall lie.

Ah! My virginity remains,
For this your mourning render now.
A man I shall not know or love,
Nor he my kiss upon the brow.

'Twas father's vow when he went forth
A sacrifice he'd offer up,
To celebrate a vict'ry won
Ere food he tasted or the cup.

So little had he thought or dreamed
'Twould be myself, nor beast nor pet,
That first appeared from out the door
And all his anguished vision met.

But kindly he then granted me
These days, these months for me to mourn,
Before my lissome body lies
Upon a burning altar, torn. _SACRIFICE

She requested 2 months to go off to roam the hills and weep with my friends, because I will Never marry.

Lissom' ✓
Thin, supple, graceful

Ruth—She Was One of Us

(Ruth 1-4)

A child was born some time ago
Right here in Bethlehem,
And people still relate this tale
Which quite astonished them.

When famine had reduced the land
And people everywhere
Were forced to seek their food abroad
In hopes they'd find it there,

"Twas then Naomi with her house
To Moab took her leave,
Expecting to improve their lot
And their distress relieve.

And many saw her when she left
With husband virile and strong.
They ventured far to foreign land
And took their sons along.

But shortly then her husband died
And she was left alone,
Except for two young sons she had
And nothing else to own.

Now for a while she lived in hope
For each son took a wife,

But when her sons themselves then died
A pall came o'er her life.

a dark
Cloud a a
Towering
smoke a
Dust

And Orpah was a daughter while
The other was named Ruth.
And in that land the Jews were few,
And neither was in truth.

About that time she heard that God
Had eased his people's lot.
In Judah there was hope once more,
In Moab there was not.

She set her face for home again
And to her daughters said,
"Remain here with your people now,
For my two sons are dead.

"I thank you for your love to them
And how you kept your oath.
May God now show you kindness and
Most richly bless you both.

"And may you other husbands find
And safely once again
Abide within a fruitful home
And bear your children then.

"My life is bitter for the hand
Of God opposes me,
And if you choose to follow now
The worse for you 'twill be."

So Orpah then her mother kissed
While bidding her good-by,

But Ruth embraced Naomi and
In whispers did reply,

"Entreat me not, O mother dear,
Your presence now to flee,
For more are you to me than what
A man might ever be.

"Entreat me not to turn as those
Of lesser love would do,
My foot withholding from the path
And leave pursuing you.

"The God I've known to be your God
Shall be my God as well.
Your people shall be mine and where
You find your home I'll dwell.

"And when death's darksome voice may call,
Entreat me not I say,
For there content, fulfilled, expired,
My body will they lay.

"And naught but death shall separate
My clinging soul from you.
May God do so and more to me
If e'er I prove untrue."

And thus they went to Bethlehem,
Inseparable as one.
The Moabitess was seen there
But of the family none.

And some, recalling well the day
She left, then said aloud,

"Can this whom now our eyes behold
Be she who left so proud?"

"Say not 'Naomi,'" she replied,
"Which speaks of pleasant fame.
For God has lifted up his hand
And bitter is my name.

"I left so full long years ago
And now I have returned.
Affliction is my lot from God
Who all my pleas has spurned."

Now barley ripened gold and full
And to the fields she went,
This Ruth in hopes she'd glean a bit
Ere harvest time was spent.

And though 'twas thought God did forsake
This lonely, weary pair,
His caring hand was not withdrawn,
In truth had led her there.

For in the fields of Boaz did
She find herself that day,
Who, when he learned just who she was,
Invited her to stay.

He was a man of honor and
Forbade his men to touch
This winsome lass of foreign birth
Of whom he'd heard so much.

And when she questioned how it was
Such favor he had shown,

"Naomi you have loved," he said,
"'Tis now quite widely known,

"And what you've done for her and how
You left your home behind,
And chose this land to make your own
And here your fate to find.

"May God beneath whose wings you're found,
Now all your efforts bless,
For kindness to our sister shown
Midst sorrow and distress."

At home that night Naomi learned
How Boaz had embraced
Her daughter Ruth and kept her from
The dangers she had faced.

She saw the mighty hand of God
At work once more therein,
And offered praise and thanks to him,
For Boaz was her kin!

"Return again," she said to Ruth,
"And listen to me now,
For Boaz is redeemer-kin
And if you will allow,

"It's in our hands to work things and
To open wide his eyes,
Assisting every effort that
Will help him win this prize!

"Tonight you'll sleep right at his feet
And when he wakens say,

'Please spread your garment over me,
As kin now let me stay.'"

So quickly to the threshing floor
Ruth hastened to obey,
And quietly she stole inside
And at his feet then lay.

And when discovered she replied
Just as Naomi said.
As kin he had redeemer rights
To purchase her and wed.

"Oh, noble woman," Boaz said,
"Quite justly is your name
Revered among our townsmen since
That blessed day you came.

"You've followed not in chase of men
Of younger age than I,
Nor sought them whether rich or poor
Their wants to gratify.

"Though foreign born you've led a life
Both wise and virtuous,
A child of Abraham in truth
And you are one of us.

"But now I tell you of a man
With closer blood than mine,
Whose right it is to purchase you
If he will so incline."

So Boaz met the man before
The elders and in brief,

The man renounced all right to Ruth,
(Which caused no small relief!),

A wedding followed shortly then,
When Boaz took her hand.
And ne'er was seen a greater feast
They say, throughout the land.

And blessed were they by elders and,
The women of the place,
Who prayed their union would be strong
And offspring thus embrace.

Now God who hears each humble prayer
And turns away not one,
Most clearly heard those ardent pleas
And granted them a son.

And from that line then came to us
A man who in our lore
Stands tall above all others as
A prince and man of war.

Yes, David was descended from
This strange, unlikely pair,
Whose son, the prophets have foretold,
Messiah's crown would wear.

Hannah's Song

(1 Sam. 1, 2)

[handwritten annotations: Wife of Elkanah / Other wife is Peninnah / Hannah-no children / Peninnah had children / Later Hannah bore Samuel & 3 sons & daughter,]

A prayer from deep within her soul
Ascended to the throne
Where God in majesty prevailed,
In hopes that he would own,

This forlorn woman's ardent plea
That she might bear a son,
And of her scornful barrenness
And ridicule be done.

Can God his children e'er deny,
Does he in truth have choice,
Entreated thus so helplessly
When by the faintest voice?

And weaned young Samuel took his place
And spent his youthful days
Within the temple, thence to bear
The God of Israel praise.

And Hannah, once her prayer appeased,
Broke forth in joyful song,
Which kindles still in grateful hearts
And shall for ages long.

My heart rejoices in the Lord,
My horn is lifted high,

And o'er the enemy I boast
Whose fateful end is nigh.

There is no other Holy One,
No Rock who can compare
With you, O Lord, who stand alone
And heav'n's bright raiment wear.

Let not proud men with loosened tongues
Now arrogantly prate,
For he who knows all things one day
Will justify their fate.

The warriors' bows has he destroyed,
But those who stumbled find
With strength renewed God lifted them
And to their needs inclined.

And those who were of stomach full
And by their palates led,
Now sell themselves despondently
And labor for their bread.

The hungry feel the pangs no more
Of emptiness and thirst,
For God their plight has kindly seen
And all their fate reversed.

The barren one of children now
No less then sev'n has borne,
But she once ringed by many sons
Alone at last will mourn.

The Lord is he who death refers,
Who makes alive again,

And whether Sheol or life beyond
He renders the Amen.

For poverty and wealth alike
Are by his hand bestowed.
The humbled and exalted thus
Are to his preference owed.

And from the dust the poor are raised,
From ash heaps those in need.
He seats them 'longside princes fair
And those of noble breed.

The earth's foundations are his own,
On them the world is set.
The feet of all his saints he guards
And stills the wicked yet.

For not by strength does one prevail.
Whoe'er shall God oppose,
His thundering voice at judgment will
Their wanton deeds expose.

But to the king shall strength be giv'n
In every wanting day.
The horn of God's anointed is
Exalted now and aye.

Samuel's Wife

Song Hannah

Her thoughts on raising 2 'naughty' sons with Samuel being around. Her lonliness & hurt & possibly resentment.

(1 Sam. 8)

A child of promise and of prayer,
This Samuel, husband, prophet, priest.
They praised him highly as they ought,
For one so honored now deceased.

Yes Israel came respects to pay,
Through many'a year they'd heard him well.
But out of sight the prophet's words,
Alas! It seemed on deaf ears fell.

But gathered here in Ramah where
They laid him deep within the ground
They mourn, they weep, they plead with God
And to the heav'ns their cries resound.

Their chanting I can hardly bear,
I'll seek a place of quietude,
Returning when the horde is gone
To mourn again in solitude.

And much there is to mourn for him,
A man of God, a father, saint.
He served his people ever well
And gave himself without restraint.

They spoke kind words of him who died.
Through him, they said, God spoke his word.

They mentioned not how their own ways
They followed still and much preferred.

Each step along this stone-filled path
Brings pain to my most swollen feet.
But I must walk until I find
Some rocky ledge for my retreat.

They'll call me now a widow but
In truth what other life was mine
Those many years I sat alone
At home to wait, to pray and pine?

At last! In this secluded place
Away from eulogies and all,
My mem'ry turns to other things
From years gone by that I recall.

Yes, more there is that could be said
Of Samuel and of me his wife,
Of how things were within the home,
Of how I suffered midst the strife.

You think me lonely now, dear friend?
I was since first I wed the man,
For God, he thought, had called him to
Address all peoples in the clan.

And thus he made the rounds each year
To Bethel, Gilgal, Mizpah too,
But how we needed him at home
His family duties to renew!

For he was not the cause of strife,
'Twas rather that he was away,

And two rebellious sons I raised
Who would not listen or obey.

I taught them all I knew but they
Together merely chided me.
A stronger hand was needed that
Respect they'd learn in some degree.

I spoke my will to Samuel oft
But he was firm in his intent
To speak his message far and wide,
That Israel of her sins repent.

And year by year I saw them grow,
My sons, without a father home.
So free to live by nature's bent
And where their natures cared to roam.

And though they followed not the Lord
In word or thought, less in each deed,
Their father made them judges who
Our holy Law should ever heed.

The people then rebelled and said
They wished to have a king to rule,
Like other nations they would be,
With throne and trappings, royal mule.

And so my sons caused further wrath
When Israel thus embraced this plea.
And finally then, I set my mind
To ask just how things came to be.

Does God call men from family ties?
Would he neglect the home indeed?

Ought not his work be done without
Removing fathers from their seed?

When sons know not a father's hand
Behind each parent's guiding word,
Will they not soon some freedom take
And disregard all that they've heard?

For that is how it was with mine.
They knew just what their father brought
To all our people so in need,
And how each day the battle fought.

But little heed they gave to him
Though he could turn a nation round.
They chose a path far from the Lord
And thought a better life they'd found.

And what if Samuel while at home
Had spent more hours with those two,
And talked to them, encouraged them
As real fathers used to do?

No poet e'er will sing my praise
Nor will my name be writ in prose,
Alone within my house I'll sit
As daily my resentment grows.

A nation would I sacrifice
That my two sons their God had sought.
But was it Samuel or God
Who for my sons gave little thought?

Unanswered question
Bewildered

Michal—Daughter of Saul

handwritten annotation: 1 Sam. 18:17 Merab daughter of Saul 1 Sam 18:20 Michal 2ND Sam 6:16

(1 Sam. 18; 2 Sam. 6)

Now judge my right to know, good friend,
If for these years I've suffered long,
While knowing neither love nor child,
By night no husband's voice or song.

Was it a sentence merited
By deeds I did or failed to do?
Now judge I say, your prudent word
May all my sorrow yet subdue.

***

I looked upon him loving much
And to my father made it known.
I was in love with David and
Would he, the king, this warrior own?

Would he invite him as a son
To be my husband, strong and fine?
Would he unite us man and wife,
And further thus the royal line?

The king announced his pleasure and
When told my David then demurred.
"I'm but a poor man to this day
And few have of my exploits heard."

The king then sent his men once more
Who said to David, "This alone
Will Saul require for your right
To Michal wed and thus to own:

"A hundred foreskins from our foe,
The Philistines along the coast."
And David thought the offer fair,
'Twould be a thing of which to boast.

But little did he understand
My father's motive nor did I,
Requesting that he do this thing
And in the face of danger fly.

My father thought this onerous task
Was quite beyond young David's skill.
The Philistines would rise up strong
And finally this pretender kill.

But twice the number asked of him
Were brought and laid at father's feet.
Thus I as wife was given him
That vows their final end would meet.

Now oft as David took up arms
And led his warriors 'gainst the foe
His God was with him mightily
And chose a vict'ry to bestow.

I heard the voice of cheering throngs,
"His thousands has King Saul now slain,
And David his ten thousands," while
The city echoed this refrain.

And need I say, from those days on
My love for David all could tell,
But with his triumphs in the field
Great fear upon my father fell.

And so the day arrived when men
Were sent to watch our house by morn.
They meant to kill my husband who
I hastened quickly to forewarn.

Then through a window he escaped
To seek another fate instead.
I took an idol and goat's hair
And told the men, "He's sick in bed."

They came again with orders to
Remove young David bed and all,
And bear him to the king that there
From shortened neck his head might fall.

The king then asked me why I would
My loyalty to him forsake.
I told him I was forced to lie
Or David my sweet life would take.

Now David was quite fair of face,
'Mongst soldiers quite above the lot,
A heart much like the Lord's, I'd heard,
Though of his faith I'd not been taught.

I waited for some years in hopes
That he returning might once more
Embrace me as his wife but naught
Was I to hear save tales of war.

My father sought him high and low
And wished to kill him, thus to end
The challenge to the throne he was,
    Considered now no royal friend.

And finally I was given to
Another man his wife to be.
My father did this out of spite
Without, of course, consulting me.

The years continued as they will,
And David got the upper hand,
In Hebron first, and Judah then
O'er all of Israel in command.

'Twas then I knew he'd not forgot
This lady, princess, cast off wife.
He sent for me to be with him
Now that he'd ended years of strife.

But were they ended? Judge, I say,
And tell me true just what you think,
That from your counsel I may learn
And of my fate more fully drink.

A celebration he proclaimed
To bring the ark of God within
Jerus'lem's gates that worship there
Both true and holy might begin.

With music, trumpets, castanets,
The people swirled without a stop,
Rejoicing in that ark of lore
And dancing till, it seemed, they'd drop.

And who should lead that loud parade?
'Twas David, he of royal fame.
He danced before the frenzied throng
And brought discredit to his name.

For I beheld though distantly,
From out a window and quite high.
I saw his every movement and
I watched him as he happened nigh.

No, I was not a part of this.
My father had not taught me so.
I knew but little of the ark,
And less its power o'er the foe.

And so it was, within my heart
I then despised my husband for
The utter crudeness he displayed.
He danced and maidens' gazes bore!

I met him ere he reached our home,
I spoke as frankly as I knew.
"And how distinguished you've become,
'Mongst servants and your retinue!

"The king is now exalted for
Disrobing thus in sight of all.
What shame, this vulgar spectacle!
How great from honor is your fall!"

In but a moment David said,
"Before the Lord I danced today.
He chose me over Saul to rule,
O'er Israel's people to hold sway.

"Before him I will dance again,
And yet more "vulgar" will I be.
My servants though, in high esteem
Will hold me as they bow the knee."

My father's line was then cut off,
No heir of his would rule the throne.
For I, you see, was put aside
No pleasure as a wife to own.

***

And thus things went within my life.
Now have you heard my tale quite well?
Then what, dear friend, do you conclude?
And I will listen as you tell.

Abigail—A Kinder, Happier Fate

means 'my father's joy'

(1 Sam. 25)

A woman of more charm and wit
Than any you might hail
In Carmel or surrounding towns,
Was beauteous Abigail.

And known as well for wisdom and
For goodness through and through,
The poor went not away denied,
Her kindness always knew.

Throughout her domicile she reigned,
A queen as all could tell,
Beloved by servants and by kin,
Revered by them as well.

But sadly she was married to
A man of foolish ilk *what elders were*
Who loved his rowdy feasts, his drink,
His garments of fine silk.

And wealth beyond compare he had,
Of sheep and goats no end,
On land extending far beyond
Where hill and plain would blend.

And why, some asked, did she consent
This man to call her mate?

For with her charms she merited
A kinder, happier fate.

And now another virtue I
Will state that may explain
Just why she chose to marry him
And as his wife remain.

A life of earnest faith she led
In hopes that one day he
Would waken to the voice of God
And all his folly see.

And as the years passed slowly by
And little change she knew,
Her hopes began to dim somewhat
As hopes denied will do.

And thus resigned she lived with him,
And often sought excuse
For boorish actions, drinking and
Continual abuse.

She finally wondered if God's plan
She had misunderstood,
For nothing less did she desire
And trusted it was good.

But then one day a servant came
Quite breathlessly to say
In distant field he worked where he
Was shearing sheep that day,

With Nabal (spouse of Abigail),
When suddenly certain men

Appeared and asked for food and drink,
And numbered fully ten.

"And these were men from David's camp,"
The servant then affirmed,
"Who in the past our safety had
Without a loss confirmed.

"But now in need and seeing beasts
Throughout our master's land,
Had come imploring meekly for
Whatever was at hand."

"'And who is David,' Nabal said,
'That I should give him food,
And who this son of Jesse now?'
He asked in peevish mood.

"And none among your servants has
A word to Nabal said,
Or e'er been able to persuade
This man so poorly bred.

"I greatly fear," the servant said,
"That vengeance now is due,
For surely David will return
And bring his army too!"

And quickly then, did Abigail
Perceive the peril and
A gala feast for David was
Prepared at her command.

Thus wine and bread and roasted grain,
And sheep well-stuffed and dressed,

And fig and raisin cakes as well,
In truth all that was best,

She loaded fast upon some mules
And straightway then set out,
To see if with God's help she might
Prevent a bloody rout.

And this she did in secret for
If Nabal were aware,
He would have overruled his wife
And stopped things then and there.

And so it was she met him as
He led the men astride,
Full bent on taking vengeance for
His humble plea denied.

And Abigail bowed low in hopes
This slaughter to deter,
And pleaded that the blame might fall
Not on her spouse but her.

"I saw them not when they appeared,
Your men so kindly sent.
Had I been there no doubt I would
All that they asked have lent.

"And Nabal as his name implies,
A fool he is at heart.
But let not vengeance guide you now
Nor ever be your part.

"The Lord has graciously restrained
Your hand from doing wrong,

And may you ever triumph and
Proclaim the victor's song.

"Now let this gift, my lord, appease
Your men who for blood shed,
Will not bear guilt as in your path
They turn aside instead.

"And when in time the Lord has done
All that to you he's vowed,
Remember then your servant here,
On bended knee and bowed."

And David was quite taken as
She humbly sought his grace,
Nor was he yet unmindful of
Her kind and lovely face.

"Now praise to God," he answered her,
"For he has sent you nigh,
And all your people kept this day
Who were about to die.

"For with four hundred men I thought
By midnight to arrive,
And truly by dawn's light there'd be
No male left alive.

"And may God's blessing be on you
For judgment shown as well,
And thus I've not offended him,
The God of Israel!"

And David turned with all his men
Who that night feasted well,

While Abigail sought out her spouse
Their perilous state to tell. *Tell Nabal*

She found him feasting and quite drunk,
As in a stupor grand,
And so she waited till the morn
That he might understand.

And then he heard how David's troop
Had come to slay the lot,
And how save by his wife's bold plan
His life would now be naught.

Then at these words this churlish man *rude, mean*
Fell straightway to the ground.
His selfish life began to ebb
And soon no more was found.

Now David waited not the day
His nation's crown to see.
He sent at once to Abigail
That she his wife might be.

And all her wealth she shared with him
As every woman does,
But greater was the wealth she brought
By who she ever was.

Bathsheba

(2 Sam. 11, 12)

I woke as sunlight ended night
And hailed each silent day,
Awaiting him from fields of war
In hopes he'd finally stay.

And oft I'd wait while scanning well
The distant hills or plain,
That I, by chance some modest glimpse
Might of his semblance gain.

Among the mighty was he named
In David's awesome force.
And few compared with shield and bow,
Afoot or on his horse.

Uriah, my Uriah, how
The very sight of you
Would all my soul full satisfy
And then my body, too!

And quite aware was I that you,
Were equal in desire,
For me and all my luring charms —
We shared a common fire.

And men with darting eyes as keen
As my Uriah's were,

Beheld my winsome form and face
Which set their tongues astir.

Yes I was known both here and yon
For loveliness and grace,
But never did I flaunt myself
In scanty garb of lace.

For one and all were soon to know
Uriah was my man,
With few who equaled him in might,
A prince within the clan.

I knew my duties as I wished
A prudent wife to be,
Observing closely all the rules
Of wifely modesty.

And thus each eve when sun had set
And darkness shielded me,
I'd bathe atop our cloistered roof
Expecting none to see.

And so, suspecting naught one day,
A knock upon the door
I answered and beheld a man
Who forthright did implore,

That I at once my house might leave
And him accompany
To David's royal house for lo,
The king had beckoned me!

I wondered why he sent for me,
No friendship did we share.

Then why? My curious mind inquired,
And soon I was aware.

For not to rooms where guests abode
Was I then quickly led,
But to an inner, private place
And to his very bed.

I knew at once why I was called,
I knew so very well,
But how could I Uriah face
And what to him then tell?

This man was he of whom I'd heard
He'd slain his thousands and
My husband often said there was
None greater in the land.

And of him also had he said
He'd follow each command,
And standing there this king of me
My body did demand.

I hurried from the palace gates,
Each step a wavering thrust,
And strangely darkened was my soul,
My heart within me crushed.

And entering my empty home
A loneliness I felt.
I sensed my God more distant now,
Nor surcease when I knelt. *Without stopping*

Uriah! My Uriah, how
The very thought of you

Brought pain that you might think at last
My love had not been true.

But then I ask, was there a choice
While standing face to face,
Or as I lay beside him there
Or in his tight embrace?

Could I deny this king his wish,
This sovereign man of war?
Had any woman so abjured
Of all who came before?

[handwritten margin note: solemnly renounce a Belief, cause, or Claim]

The weeks and months passed torturously
And then one day I knew,
I was with child from David's seed
As deep within I grew.

I sent this word to David then,
Expecting some reply,
But silence was his answer to
My furtive, helpless cry.

I feared each day might be the one
Uriah would appear,
Yet longed for him to understand,
To comfort and be near.

And then one morn I suddenly heard,
He had returned at last!
Should I assume he nothing knew,
Or tell him of the past?

I waited and was torn within,
What plea was I to make?

Would he most kindly understand
And call it "a mistake"?

Or would he harshly judge my sin
And charge me as a wife,
Unfaithful like a harlot and
Unfit to share his life?

I waited as the day drew on
And through the lonely night,
But saw him not nor heard his voice
By morning's first pale light.

And had he learned somehow that I
Had with his captain lain,
While he bore sword and shield in hand
And fought across the plain?

Was this the reason that he chose
To see me not that night,
Preferring solitude elsewhere
And then returned to fight?

But soon these thoughts were banished when
A messenger there came
Who told me of Uriah's death
Upholding David's name.

Uriah, my Uriah, how
With every memory
My heart in anguish longs for you
And what you were to me!

And if you knew did you forgive?
If not then did you die

Believing still, though distantly,
My love was ever nigh?

And mourning thus one barren day
A knock there came once more,
A man in royal trappings stood
Before my well-worn door.

"Twas he with whom I'd spent the night
When I of sense did flee,
And what, I asked, could he now want,
And what more ask of me?

Tamar—Most Favored Once

(2 Sam. 13)

Most favored once, I walked within
My father's house serene, content.
My beauty was a thing well known
And caused no loathing or dissent.

For all my father's ways I sought
To keep within a humble heart,
To serve the king, his bidding do,
Fulfilled my life in whole and part.

But lest you think within that life
No harm or heartbreak could befall,
I tell you now of what occurred
As warning both to you and all.

I was a virgin daughter of
King David, Israel's Chosen One,
And honored in his household though
Without the fanfare of a son.

One day my father made of me
This kind request for Amnon who
Lay sick and would not eat save I
Prepare some bread without ado.

In innocence and quick to serve
I baked the meal before his eyes.

I served it warm that he might eat,
And then to my unfeigned surprise,

He ordered all to leave the room
And beck'ning me close to his bed,
With sudden strength he reached his hand,
But not for fresh, appealing bread!

No, I was what he had desired.
And then 'twas clear, he was not sick.
He'd planned from end to fateful end
This cruel and shocking, lowly trick.

"Now force me not," I pleaded loud,
"In Israel things are not thus done.
"'Tis wicked what you wish to do,
E'en for yourself a king's first son.

"And you, my brother, would be shamed
Like one of Israel's discontents.
And what disgrace would still be mine
Though after countless sore laments.

"But speak a word now to the king
For surely he will not withhold
My hand in marriage from his son,
Nor reprimand you nor yet scold."

But he heard not a word I said
So deep, so frenzied his desire.
He grabbed me and his strength prevailed
Till spent each vestige of his fire.

'Twas done, the deed forever sealed,
And lo! The change that o'er him came!

His love replaced by hatred now
As if on me fell all the blame.

No scorn had I so merited
As he then heaped upon my name.
He ordered me to leave his home
As if my presence brought it shame.

And still I thought there might be hope,
Despite this travesty we could
Some honor salvage through it all,
Some bit of decency, some good.

"Send not this sister from your house
For that, my brother, would be worse
Than all that you have done to me
In bringing down this vile curse."

But once again he heard me not
And calling to a servant there,
He ordered I be carried out
Thus ending his short-lived affair.

"Be sure you bolt the door," he said,
"Lest she return and further bring
Disgrace upon disgrace to me,
A prince, the heir, son of the king."

I tore my virgin's garment well
And left with ashes on my head.
My moans and cries were heard afar
As o'er the downward path I fled.

"Oh, Absalom!" I called when near
This brother's place of refuge then,

And with a single look he knew
I'd just escaped some lecher's den.

He asked if it was Amnon who
Indulged himself and honor stole.
He asked but knew the answer well
And vowed some vengeance in his soul.

*****

And now two years have fully passed,
I wait within this brother's place.
The king has known of Amnon's deed
But calls him not his sin to face.

Abandoned, without hope some man
Will seek me for his wife one day,
My beauty slowly fades and yet
The violent, piercing memories stay.

Has Absalom forgotten now?
He's gone afar to shear his sheep.
He'll have a feast with brothers all,
Will he some retribution seek?

But I shall be content with none,
No vengeance have I ever sought.
From youth I was instructed well
To keep the ways my father taught.

A Noble Wife

More precious than bright rubies is
A wife of noble character,
And he who searches well will find
He nothing lacks with her.

Full confident he is that she
Will do him ever good not harm.
With eager hands she serves his needs,
His ardor with her charm.

And wool and flax for children's garb
That clothed in raiment they might be,
Are neatly spun by distaff and
Full spindle on her knee.

She brings from ports afar her goods
And sweet the table that she lays,
Which early rising she prepares,
And loving care betrays.

And portions for her servant girls
Are never lacking for she knows
With willing hearts they serve the home,
And much to them she owes.

She wisely trades and profit gains
Then ponders well a distant field,

Exploring reasons for, against,
And buys it for its yield.

And with her earnings then she plants
A vineyard on its gentle slopes,
And for a harvest rich and full
She confidently hopes.

Her arms for all her tasks are strong,
Her work with love and vigor done.
Her lamp burns long through many a night
Beyond the setting sun.

The poor are welcomed to her home
And leave not unattended for
"Tis known by all that none has e'er
In vain approached her door.

And winter? Little fear she has
Of swirling wind or stabbing cold,
For all her children scarlet-clad,
Its wondrous sights behold.

Her bed is overlaid 'gainst chill,
And clothed in linen garments fine
She greets her husband, proud, content,
And sits with him to dine.

And he when seated at the gates
With those who in the city dwell,
Finds high regard 'mongst elders there
From friend and foe as well.

Both strength and dignity are hers
As wisely she her part displays,

Her care for household matters such
She laughs at evil days.

Her children rise and call her blest
For by her love they prosper well,
Her husband too in joyous voice
Waits not her praise to tell.

"Of women found throughout the land
Who noble deeds are wont to do,
For all your works and all you are
None have compared with you."

Now charm misleads the heart of man,
And beauty graces but the young,
Yet she who fears the Lord in truth,
Her praise will e'er be sung.

And gather then, both one and all
Where'er 'tis fitting that we be,
To praise this woman, mother, wife
In seemly, apt degree!

Jezebel—She Led a Nation

(1 Kgs. 16-21)

The daughter of a king was she,
This Jezebel of whom I speak,
And foreign born, who could have thought
What harm in Israel she would wreak?

She cast her lot with Ahab and
As queen within our land knew not
Restraint in turning Israel's clan
To idols we for long had fought.

She urged him on in wicked ways,
And who in truth ruled from the throne
Was doubtful though it mattered not,
By both were seeds of evil sown.

She ruled her husband till he would
In sin all men of lore excel.
While Baal's prophets swelled their ranks
And those of Asherah as well.

For hundreds of these prophets ate
At tables served by Jezebel,
And rising then, false gods they preached
With words resounding like a knell.

At nothing would she stop to turn
Our people's hearts from God's true way.

The prophets of the Lord she bound,
To end their teaching and to slay.

E'en to Elijah, prophet, priest,
Her vilest threats were manifest,
For when he finished with the sword
Her prophets, humbled on the crest,

She sent this chilling word to him,
"Now be assured by this dark hour
Tomorrow will I make your life
Like one of them in death's cruel power."

And such the fear she raised in him
That for his very life he ran,
And in a desert waste he prayed
To join his long departed clan.

The lowly also knew her scorn
And here I speak of Naboth who
A vineyard owned, lush and serene,
Each morn enriched by sun and dew.

Now Ahab coveted the place
And wished to buy or trade for it,
But Naboth chose to keep the land
Nor would he any loss permit.

So Ahab mourned and sulked at home,
He would not eat and lay in bed.
But Jezebel learned what occurred
And Naboth then, was good as dead.

"Is this the way a king should act?
The man who rules in Israel?

Now rise, cheer up!" she said, "You'll have
The vineyard of that infidel."

(And are you now more prone to see
The evil that in Jezebel
At any moment might arise?
But wait, there's more I have to tell.)

She ordered that a feast be held
And Naboth would be honored there.
"But seat two scoundrels at his side
That they may confidently swear,

"They heard the man curse God and king.
And for this act he must be stoned
By elders, nobles and the rest
For such audacity he owned."

The feast was held, the scoundrels hired
And all things went as she had planned.
She told the king, "Your foe is dead,
His blood now stains the burning sand."

So Ahab rose from off his bed
To see the place his wife had got.
But what he did displeased the Lord,
And all the queen's malicious plot.

The Lord then sent Elijah and
A prophecy of doom he told,
Concerning Ahab and his wife
Who had their hearts so vilely sold,

To bring such evil to the land,
To Israel's chosen, suffering race.

A shocking end they each would know,
Nor royal heirs would they embrace.

Now later Jehu reigned as king,
And Jezebel's foreseen demise
Drew daily nearer, yet would she
Not from her evil ways arise.

And as the king marched through the town
Our lady from a window saw
His entourage, his troops aligned,
And felt contempt but little awe.

Her eyes were painted brazenly
And like a vulture she appeared.
Her hair was set in braids and with
Some cheap and pungent unguent smeared.

Her visage was exceeded by
The words she shouted to the king,
And they, for all their untamed scorn,
Her final end would shortly bring.

She asked if he had come in peace,
This errant queen, this scheming one.
She called him by the tarnished name
Of Zimri who had murder done.

The king, offended greatly, called
Upon his servants at her side
To cast poor Jezebel head first
From out the window where she died,

As horses at their masters' word
Pranced over her with hooves brought high.

Her wailing ended soon for she
Had long been destined thus to die.

Her blood was spattered 'gainst a wall
And wandering dogs soon found her there.
They left but hands and feet and skull
Before returning to their lair.

'Twas Jehu then who uttered words
Elijah first to all had said,
That Jezreel's dogs would eat the flesh
Of Jezebel when she was dead.

This woman was a sinner, true,
But many others have there been.
So why this harshest judgment now?
She led a nation into sin.

A Widow's Plea

(2 Kgs. 4)

In ancient Israel's land there lived,
A widow with her boys,
Both fatherless and penniless
And few their daily joys.

For though the father had revered
The Lord in every way,
His gift was not to save a coin
Nor growing debts repay.

And when expired he left behind
An ample sum quite due,
Which sons and mother could not pay
And daily only grew.

The creditor then sent this word
Since she could not comply,
Advising her in sternest tones
To bid her sons goodbye.

For he would make of them his slaves,
Quite legally approved,
So having lost her husband now,
Her sons would be removed.

In desperation then she turned
Most urgently to plead

That blest Elisha bend his ear
And kindly intercede.

"And what is found within your house?"
The prophet asked of her.
She answered, "Naught but meager oil
I have at home, kind sir."

"Now go," he said, "and of your friends,
Each woman, every man,
For jars that they may lend inquire
And gather all you can.

"Take every vessel to your home
And when you've closed the door,
With only your two sons beside
Proceed the oil to pour."

Now she had learned to listen well
When prophets were inclined
To speak a word from God that might
Reveal what he designed.

And soon she learned just what he planned,
How kind his mercies are,
As endlessly the stream of oil
She poured to fill each jar,

And only took her rest at last
When there remained not one
Among the jars as yet unfilled,
Brought in by either son.

And there before her she beheld
In vessels running o'er,

God's rich provision for her plight
That covered all the floor.

She hastened to Elisha then
And told him what occurred.
And calmly this great man of God
Then spoke to her this word,

"Now sell all that you need to pay
The debts your husband left,
That you may not this day be found
Of home and sons bereft."

Then joyously the widow turned
And joined her sons once more.
They last were seen with arms upraised
Within the temple door.

A Hebrew Servant Girl

(2 Kgs. 5)

I live afar from home once known
Nor ever had I thought to stray,
But when a raiding troop came forth
As swift as desert winds one day,

I found 'twas useless that I fled
In hopes I might some refuge find,
For horse and rider sought me out
As if to me alone assigned.

And to this land of Aram then,
They carried me through many'a day,
While heeding not my urgent pleas
Nor tears I shed in my dismay.

Now Naaman was commander of
The troop that day that brought such strife,
Who over all the army ruled,
And I was brought to serve his wife.

A maiden and of Israel's stock,
My chores were done, both large and small,
And I was treated in this home
With kind regard by one and all.

I was allowed to keep my faith
While others went their chosen way,

For early had my parents taught
The Lord was he to whom we pray.

But soon a sadness lingered o'er
My life each day, weighed down with grief
For Naaman, master, had been struck
With leprosy beyond relief.

And none within this land could find
A cure that might restore his health,
Though some their gods of stone implored
In hopes to somehow share his wealth.

The day arrived when I approached
My mistress with this solemn plea:
"If Naaman would to Israel go
A cure he'd find for leprosy,

"For there a prophet yet abides
Within a modest northern town,
Who serves the Lord Almighty nor
Will on a man's petition frown."

Well, she to Naaman passed this word
And then, (oh wonder!) he inclined
To seek the king's permission that
In Israel's land some cure he'd find.

He left and now I hasten to
The end of what I have to tell,
For just this morning he returned
And from his leprosy is well!

His skin as smooth as mine appears,
Or should I say much like a boy's.

No longer sad he jokes and laughs
And every passing hour enjoys.

His servants say he first refused,
So simple was the prophet's word,
And was prepared to leave the place
For what he thought just too absurd.

But one convinced him to obey
For prophets should not be ignored.
In Jordan's waters then he dipped
Full seven times and was restored!

He offered many gifts for what
The prophet through his God had done.
"I serve the Lord alone," he heard,
"And of your gifts I need not one."

"There is no God," my master said,
"In all the world like Israel's God.
Henceforth I swear, my sacrifice
Will be to him on holy sod."

And to fulfill this solemn vow
He's brought with him from that far place
Two loads of earth on which to kneel
And there his new-found God embrace.

And finally I have understood
Just why to me such pain befell,
And why a sovereign God saw fit
That I in pagan lands should dwell.

Esther

(Esther 1-10)

Now Xerxes king of Persia ruled
From Susa's citadel,
And I as queen thought surely I
Would e'er in safety dwell.

A hundred provinces and more
From Cush to India's land,
He ruled and there was not a foe
Who dared to raise a hand.

And he had chosen me among
The loveliest and best,
That on my fair and comely head
A regal crown should rest.

For Vashti who was first to reign
Beside him on the throne,
Displeased the king and all his men
For her contempt once shown,

Refusing a request that he
Quite drunk had made one day,
That she in royal robes appear,
As if there on display.

And for this deed she was removed.
The king would search again

For yet a lovelier, better queen,
As counseled by his men.

And when they chose me to appear
'Mongst women not a few,
I told them not whence I had come
Nor that I was a Jew.

For Mordecai, a cousin, had
Advised me in this way.
More like a father he had been
If truth one were to say.

I was assigned fair maidens who
Would tend to all my need,
And thus within the palace walls
For nothing had to plead.

And from the day the king beheld
My form and loveliness,
He wished naught but to make me his,
And all my charms possess.

Then followed soon a marriage feast,
The king sent out a call
That nobles and officials come
To fill the banquet hall.

A holiday was then proclaimed
Throughout his many lands,
And gifts of royal origin
Were borne by many hands.

And still I not a word would say
Of who my people were,

Uncertain that my master then,
Would yet a Jew prefer.

But if in safety I had thought
I dwelt from day to day,
A word from Modecai arrived
That put me in dismay.

For Haman, 'mongst the nobles first
And by the king admired,
Was filled with hatred for my kind
And thus our end conspired.

A date was set, an edict signed,
It had the royal seal,
And laws of Persians and the Medes
Were quite without appeal.

"Now you must go before the king,"
My cousin ordered me,
"And bowing low on our behalf
Most humbly make your plea."

But I demurred, I knew so well,
Unless he called me first,
A single punishment there was
And of them all—the worst!

But Mordecai replied that day
With words I'll ne'er forget,
Which were of all he'd said to me
By far the noblest yet.

"Think not that you alone will find
Of Jews in every place

A haven from destruction that
Awaits our noble race.

"For silent, still there will arise
Deliverance for our kind,
But you and all your father's house
Will not its refuge find.

"And have you not for such a time
As this come to the throne,
And for this reason wear the crown
That you have come to own?"

And humbled then for seeking first
My safety and not theirs,
I sent him word to call a fast
And help me with his prayers!

And I before the king would go,
Disdaining thus the law,
To plead before great Xerxes' throne
In reverence and in awe.

And if it meant I perished then,
That risk I had to take.
It was a worthy sacrifice
That I was called to make.

And when the king beheld my form
In royal robes arrayed,
His scepter he then offered me
And to his presence bade.

"And what," he said, "is your request
That you have come this way?

The half of all my kingdom now,
I offer you this day."

I asked him to a banquet and
With Haman to attend,
I hoped this evil man to stop
And bring him to an end.

Then feasting well on olives, dates
And long-fermented wine,
I thought the time had come to share
The sorrow that was mine.

"And will my lord not spare my life
For which I make my plea,
And merciful, give heed to all
That has befallen me?

"And will my lord not save us from
This undeservéd end
That I and all my people face
And does our fate portend?

"For truly now in every place
Destruction is our lot,
And naught but death will finally bring
The peace we long have sought."

Enraged, with staff in hand he rose
And sternly asked of me
To name the one who sought our end
And who this man might be.

"'Tis Haman who has done it, lord,
The man at your right hand,

Who plots my people's slaughter and
Has issued the command."

And leaving then his wine, so filled
With vehemence was he,
The king gave thought to Haman and
To what his end should be.

And Haman, quite undone, then fell
Upon me where I lay,
And begged that I might mercy show
And Xerxes' wrath allay.

But Xerxes entered and beheld
This vile, intemperate man
Full prostrate over me as I
Reclined on the divan.

"And will he thus molest the queen
Within this house of mine,
Is this now what he thinks of me,
For this he came to dine?"

And with these words he ordered that
They hang poor Haman high
Upon the gallows he had made
For cousin Mordecai.

Now once the king was made aware
Of all the foes we faced
Throughout his many provinces,
He acted then with haste.

We were allowed to save ourselves,
Our properties defend,

And everywhere did vanquish and
Quite valiantly contend.

And Mordecai was recompensed
For how he helped the king,
Receiving Haman's properties
And Xerxes' signet ring.

Thus honored by the king, he was
Within the palace wall,
Excepting him who wore the crown,
Exalted over all.

The Jews in every place had cause
To feast and celebrate.
And days of Purim hence are known
Beginning with this date.

Elizabeth

The years have treated tenderly
This body aged and worn,
That bore in elder years a son
By angel vision sworn.

Yes, time had passed me by I thought
As Zechariah's wife,
To bring a child or maybe two
And joy into his life.

And for my part I also say
I longed so secretly
That God might somehow bend his ear
And hear my earnest plea.

A thousand wishes daily filled
My aching, empty soul,
For all around I heard their sounds,
As in and out they stole.

But year was added unto year
And quite without a child,
I kept my faith midst all my shame
And through it all I smiled.

Now Zeke and I were known to be
Deserving in God's sight,

His laws and regulations kept
And never hoped to slight.

From Aaron's tribe we both had come
And faithful to his call,
My husband had become a priest
And wore the cleric's shawl.

But we had prayed, nay had beseeched
So many years in vain,
I finally was quite confident
That naught would lift my pain.

And then one day my husband came,
His priestly duties done,
Assuring me most fervently
That I would have a son!

And not with words he spoke to me
When he that day had come,
But by the signs he wildly made
For he was strangely dumb.

An angel had appeared to him
Assuring of this birth,
That would to many be the cause
Of penitence and mirth.

For many he would turn to God
And great would be his fame
Before the people and the Lord,
And John would be his name.

A life of hardship and denial
Would be his calling for

Midst desert heat he'd live but not
Fermented drink e'er pour.

Instead, from birth would he be filled
By God's own Spirit and
A people for the Lord prepare
Throughout our ruined land.

And Zechariah hearing this,
In doubtful voice and meek
Then questioned what the angel said
And could no longer speak.

But I one night not long therefrom
Lay in his firm embrace,
And soon I knew a healthy boy
Would join our chosen race.

I took myself to distant hills
Awaiting our son John,
For God his favor had bestowed
And my reproach was gone!

And Mary, she of kin to me,
Arrived and when she spoke
I felt the babe within my womb
As if he then awoke,

For at the sound of her sweet voice
The babe within me leapt.
And then God's mighty Spirit came
And over me he swept.

I marveled much at seeing her
And asked how it might be

That she, the mother of my Lord,
Would thus so favor me.

"And blest," I said, "is she who heard
What God for her had willed,
And then believed that what he said
Would be in her fulfilled."

And Zechariah was restored
The day our son was born.
The bonds that had enslaved his tongue
Were from his dumb lips torn.

For though our friends and kinsmen thought
He should be named for Zeke,
His father wrote, "His name is John,"
And from that time could speak.

And when a man, John left our home
In deserts to abide,
And there began to lift his voice
As Israel's faithful guide.

Now much had been foretold of John
On whom God's mighty hand
Would rest empowering him to preach,
And 'gainst all evil stand.

As prophet of the Lord Most High
The way he would prepare,
That Israel, roused and penitent,
Might all her sins forswear,

And that salvation they would know,
From darkness find release,

And with the sun's bright rays to guide
Would tread the paths of peace.

My years are nearly finished now,
My sight has greatly waned,
But mem'ries of angelic hosts
And visions have remained.

Our son a lively youth enjoyed
And nothing we withheld.
He honored us as children ought
And all our hopes excelled.

And now content, I wait the day
The prophecies foretold,
When through his word all Israel shall
Their God once more behold.

And surely over time he'll know,
A fruitful ministry.
And how I wish a longer life
Its blessèd end to see.

Mary's Song

(Lk. 1)

She heard the angel voice announce
A child she was to bear,
Whose kingdom would no end discern
As David's royal heir.

And blest was she 'mongst women for
God favored her so well,
And Virgin Mary then began
This song of praise to tell:

My soul now magnifies the Lord,
For mindful of my state
And all my lowly circumstance
That e'er have been my fate,

He has requited mercifully
And great things he has done.
My name will generations bless,
Their voices raise as one.

His Name is holy and in him
My spirit does rejoice,
My Savior God, the Mighty One,
Whose praise this day I voice.

To those who fear him mercy shall
Their portion ever be,

But those who harbor pride within
He scatters mightily.

And rulers 'mongst the nations he
From thrones has now brought down,
But kindly does he look on those
Of humble, meek renown.

The hungry has he filled and more
With good things they required,
And empty sent the rich away,
Nor gave what they desired.

His servant Israel he has
Remembered mercifully.
And kindness has he shown to those
Of Abr'ham's progeny.

Mary, Mother of Jesus

(Lk. 1, ff.)

In Nazareth we made our home,
A distant, northern place,
Enjoying neither wealth nor fame
'Mongst others of our race.

For often was it said of us
By those who ventured near,
"Can ought but ill reside therein,
Or what is good appear?"

I pondered as my youth I passed
If ever we would sing
The praises of a Nazarene,
Some prophet, priest or king.

But other thoughts more often weighed
Upon my girlish mind,
When with my friends I spent an hour
Or solitude would find.

For Roman soldiers filled the streets,
Were seen in every place,
So haughty, boastful, swaggering,
And handsome too of face.

We saw them march about our town,
They smiled and winked an eye.

And when they whispered privately
Who wished not to comply?

We talked of this one, that one and
Another that we saw,
Of one whose eyes were almond-shaped
And one with jutting jaw.

And then there was the one so tall,
And one with shoulders broad,
But never did I hear of one
Who spoke of loving God.

And so a distance I would keep,
I went my way with care.
They knew I was a servant girl
And finely shaped and fair.

And even when in presence of
A man who was our own,
I still with circumspect behaved,
And never was alone.

A virgin was I kept in hopes
A worthy man one day
Might take me as his wife and thus,
Our poverty allay.

And so the dreams we shared as girls,
The spry, coquettish ways,
Were quite acceptable I guess,
But only for those days,

Since early were we taught to bear
For family's sake our part,

From idleness to take our leave
And youthful ways depart.

And often was I pointed to
A cousin who had wed
An older man who was a priest,
And walked with God, they said.

And as the years went by, poor souls,
They waited patiently
That God in time might bless them with
A child and family.

And so I thought their time had passed,
Would I then, find the same?
Would God from me this gift withhold,
This gift whence honor came?

But little time could I afford
To dwell on thoughts like these,
Our land was overrun by men
Who forced us to our knees.

And I with faithful Jews prayed oft
A prophet God would send,
Delivering us from foreign rule
And thus Rome's power end.

But well I knew our people had
From God departed long.
We chose to disregard his law,
Instead of right, the wrong.

Now Joseph then I met who was
Impressive in his way,

A kindly man, a carpenter,
With not a lot to say.

He traced his heritage far back
Till David's line he met,
And when in time we were betrothed
I thought my life was set.

But then one day I'll ne'er forget,
When in my duties found,
A voice I heard and when I looked
There was no one around.

And upward then I cast my eye,
In hopes my ear was true,
And saw uplifted in the sky
An angel 'gainst the blue.

And robed in light, with piercing eye
He fixed his gaze on me,
And then he spoke these gracious words
So clear and solemnly,

"Oh, Mary, highly favored one
With whom God deigns to dwell,
To you I'm sent by God Most High
These tidings now to tell.

"A son you are to bear who shall
Great David's throne ascend.
His name shall be exalted and
His kingdom never end.

"As Son of the Most High he'll rule
And Jacob's house will claim.

The Holy One of God is he,
And Jesus is his name."

And troubled then, I asked of him,
Whose presence frightened me,
"Since I no man have ever known,
How shall this come to be?"

"The Spirit of our God," he said,
"Shall hover over you.
And thus the child who shall be born
His power shall imbue.

"And now Elizabeth your kin
Who was of barren state,
Shall also have a child—with God
Naught ever proves too great."

And thus the angel left as I
In humble, full accord,
Replied, "So be it unto me,
The servant of the Lord."

I passed some days quite seriously
In quiet, sober thought,
Reflecting deeply on his words,
Those words with meaning fraught.

For what would that dear man of mine,
My Joseph, think of this,
To find that I with child was.
That I had gone amiss?

And could I hope that somehow he
Might understand just how

Quite absent his (or other's) part,
I was with child now?

And people too, would surely know
And scandal would arise.
They'd wag their tongues, besmirch my name
And wink their tickled eyes.

Bur firmly I dismissed these thoughts
For little did I care,
Since God had made of me the choice
His precious Son to bear.

Mary—
A Sword Will Pierce Your Soul

(Lk. 2, ff.)

His words foretold a fearful day,
This saintly, aged man,
I knew him not before that hour
Or how he knew God's plan.

Our son we'd brought to temple courts
The Law's demand to keep,
Thus consecrating him to God
And righteousness to reap.

And Simeon took the infant up
And praising God he said,
"Lord, let thy servant now depart,
For thou hast visited,

"Thy people Israel and hast
In sight of all to see
Prepared salvation's light to shine
That all men might be free.

"And Gentiles too, shall walk therein
For it shall be to them
A light for revelation just
As for the sons of Shem."

I wondered at those words but what
He ventured next to say
Has ever all my thoughts alarmed
Nor left me for a day.

"This child," he said, "will be a sign
That many will oppose,
And some will rise and others fall,
Their thoughts he will expose.

"And you, oh mother young and fair,
My words shall not console,
For great will be your pain one day,
A sword will pierce your soul!"

And o'er the years I questioned oft
With heart resigned and stilled,
If those morose, prophetic words
Were finally now fulfilled.

"A sword!" I heard, and yet those years
While he was but a boy
Within the home obediently
Were filled with purest joy.

A lad so bright and always fun,
So thoughtful for a youth,
Whose teasing words could bring a laugh
But never lacked in truth.

And when his brothers then were born,
And sisters followed too,
He dutif'ly their charge would take
As elder brothers do.

But as he grew in stature with
Both God and man, it seemed
He thought himself apart in ways
I never would have dreamed.

We left Jerusalem one day
And homeward then were bound.
And when we later looked for him
He nowhere could be found.

Returning then we searched three days
And finally he was found
Addressing all the elders there
Within the temple ground.

His questions stumped the best of them,
(From one so young and brave!),
But greater their surprise to hear
The answers that he gave.

And I no little bothered then
Took him aside and said,
"Now son, the way you've treated us
Bespeaks a youth ill-bred.

"And there's no doubt you knew quite well
We'd search the town for you,
So please explain to us at once,
As parents it's our due."

And then I thought a sword I felt,
For calmly he replied
That his allegiance as a son
Quite elsewhere did reside.

"And knew you not," he questioned me,
"You'd find me without doubt
Within my Father's house and there
His business be about?"

Was this the sword old Simeon meant
When Jesus, infant son,
He blessed within his arms and me
Forewarned when he was done?

But glad was I it came about,
The moment quickly passed,
And taking then his leave of all
He went with us at last.

But what he said remained with me,
Though dimly then discerned,
Those words about his "father's house"
So deeply in me burned.

And there in Nazareth we lived
And Jesus took his place,
Obedient in all things and grew
In wisdom and in grace.

Most fortunate this was for me
Since Joseph soon took ill,
And fatherless we found ourselves
According to God's will.

And for a dozen years and more
He worked his father's trade.
And houses everywhere were filled
With all the things he made.

But then one day he said goodbye,
The time was now at hand,
He must fulfill his Father's will,
And all that he had planned.

No more would he be found at home,
No more the elder son,
No more his work with wood and awl,
His life with us was done.

And oh! The pain I felt as then
Once more he pierced my heart.
And surely Simeon's words had found
Their end – in whole and part,

For well I knew, once gone there'd be
Within our house a void
Of laughter, singing, fun he brought
We daily had enjoyed.

My son! Tonight what pillow rests
Your weary tender head?
Or have you found an open field
With hard, cold rock instead?

And will the dew descending o'er
Your sleeping body there,
Bring comfort as you nightly had
Within your mother's care?

And have you found a friend or two
While wandering in your way,
Who, loving as your family did,
Prepare your meal each day?

Yes, these my prayers for you, dear son,
Shall not my lips depart,
In hope that though so very weak
They may some ease impart.

And as the aching days went by,
No longer could we stand
His loss and thus we searched for him,
If just to touch his hand.

A wedding then took place and there
I saw him once again,
But ere the chance to sit and talk
The steward and his men,

Implored that I inform my son
Of wine they had run short,
And would I kindly speak to him
Enlisting his support?

And this I did quite readily,
And quick lamented it,
For what he said rebuking me,
More painful mem'ries lit.

"Dear woman," he addressed me then,
"And why this urging so?
My time has not yet come and what
Do I to them now owe?"

And though he filled them all with wine,
(He had some pity felt),
In vain it served to lessen all
The sorrow I was dealt.

"Dear woman..." he had said to me
Who from his birth did nurse,
And hold and rock and sing to him,
And prayed when things went worse.

"Dear woman!" and was that the way
A son his mother greets?
Who longing, searching, finding, then
Is pointed to the streets?

Had things now come to this? It seemed
That prophecy of old
Had surely found a resting place,
Its grave both deep and cold.

If so then hopes at last were mine,
The sword had finally left,
And Simeon's words no more could do,
My soul was fully cleft.

We left him there in Cana with
His followers all around.
In silence I would bear my pain
As we went homeward bound.

But then one day a word we heard
Which caused no small offense.
My son was acting strange, they said,
He quite had left his sense.

We sought him once again and found
Within a house he taught,
But entrance was denied us for
The crowd his message brought.

And thinking he could ne'er forget
The years he spent with me,
Since first I nursed and sang to him
And dandled on my knee,

Most sure I was a moment he
Would take to come outside,
And greet me with his brothers there
And briefly then abide.

"Be sure you say his mother waits,"
A messenger I told,
Who brought me then my son's reply
In words quite stern and cold.

"And who is mother to me now?"
He'd said in certain tone.
"Who does my Father's will shall be
The mother that I own."

He came not out to greet me then,
I saw him not that day,
I reached for him but found instead
He turned me quite away.

And had I not the Father's will
Obeyed for all to see?
And had the angel not proclaimed
How God had favored me?

And had there ever been a time
Within our home when I
Was not attentive to his needs,
Or pained to see him cry?

And Simeon's words, prophetic now,
Were nothing but a curse,
For something yet awaited me
That surely was far worse.

I saw him from a distance for
The soldiers kept at bay
His family and his followers
That dark and final day.

The hands I'd kissed a thousand times
Were pierced as was my soul,
His feet held by a single nail
That tore a jagged hole.

And I could not prevent myself,
I slowly did approach,
In hopes I'd hear some final word
Of kindness—not reproach!

For yet I hoped he had not lost
The love I knew he had
For this poor mother all the years
I knew him as a lad.

It had to be, I told myself,
His loyalty was first
To One he called his Father not
To me who him had nursed.

Would I one final word now hear
Confirming that he cared?
Could he give thought to me just now
In all the pain he shared?

I saw his swollen lips then part
And to his follower there,
I heard this softly whispered word
That banished my despair.

"Henceforth this woman by your side
As mother you will know,
And woman," then he said to me,
"This son I now bestow."

And quickly fled my lingering doubts
But not my throbbing pain,
For lifting eyes to heav'n he prayed,
His life about to wane,

That they might be forgiven and
Of all their guilt be rid,
For in pursuing him to death
They knew not what they did.

And Simeon's meaning now was clear,
(Its quest had turned me mad,)
'Twas not my son rejected me,
In truth he never had,

But rather there to see him hang,
A spiteful death to know,
Though he had served their needs so well
And ever love would show.

And can there be a greater pain,
More vile or unjust,
Than thus to ingrates lose a son?
'Tis sure the cruelest thrust.

And to what purpose, I inquire?
Who will this act defend?
Can even God explain just why
His life came to this end?

Mary—A Maid with Favor Shown

(Acts 1, ff.)

O vaunted harbinger of fate,
Life's ultimate decree
From out your grasp has now been torn,
Where your victory?

Your sting once feared as death itself
A balm has now suppressed,
And over death our God now rules,
Bids my soul to rest.

I saw him once since that dark day,
Resplendent glory shone
Appearing to a throng as he
Rose to take his throne.

For God had raised him from the dead,
Those bonds could not contain
In darkness e'er this righteous Son,
Nor his sleep sustain.

Yes, Jesus was alive and I
Then finally, fully knew
Just why the sword had pierced so deep,
Often and so true.

'Twas what I did that caused the pain
And not his wanting love,

As all my will I vainly sought,
Not that from above.

And if a light he was to be
To Gentile and to Jew,
He first through death's dark veil would pass,
Ancient prophets knew.

And light to me he was as well,
Though favored, I had need
Of his redemption since I too,
Came of Adam's seed.

And in our home he learned to be
A Jewish boy so true,
But from another Father learned
All he was to do.

And now content I am with this:
We raised him as a son,
But knew not what the cross would mean
When his life was done.

Now daily do they come and go
To lands quite far afield,
And bear the message of his cross,
Without sword or shield.

And some bear faces rarely seen
With tongues of foreign sound,
And dress that strangely meets the eye
Everywhere is found.

But with a single message these
Are bound in love each day,

And Jesus is the one they preach
As they meet and pray.

So filled with joy, it matters not
They scarce can understand
What each dear brother next will say,
From an unknown land.

And always when they learn of me
They ask and then implore
That I might tell them of my son,
Always wanting more.

"So like a boy!" they often say
As some brief tale I share,
And then his Name exalting high,
Lord of all declare.

For in his Name invincible
They've found themselves to be,
And demons and all malady
At his Name will flee.

Could I have thought while he at home
I raised so tenderly
And taught, rebuked and then forgave,
Lord of all could be?

But that is what they say of him
And wish the world to hear,
And thus what once I pondered deep,
Finally is made clear.

I'm honored here by one and all
Just as that wintry night

I heard strange songs from high above,
        Brought to me by light.

And shepherds showed their reverence too,
        And then the Magi three,
        And who can say why privilege
        Thus should come to me?

But this alone have I desired,
        They think of me no more
Than what the'angelic host once heard
        When to him I swore,

"I'm but a maid with favor shown,
        God's servant willingly,
And wish naught but that all your words
        Be fulfilled in me."

A Woman from Samaria

(Jno. 4)

I saw him weary, resting there,
Alone as if in wait
That someone passing by the well
Might then his thirst abate.

For as each weary step I took
O'er dusty trail, I saw
No bucket did he have in hand
These waters deep to draw.

I fixed an eye most firmly on
This lonely stranger who
Beyond a doubt I knew to be
A hungry, thirsty Jew.

And would he also be inclined
As men so often were,
To flatter with his words and then
To vanquish and to slur?

Determined not to say a word
But be about my chore,
I'd fill my vessel and be gone,
And thus his need ignore.

But as my bucket found the depths
Its splashing reached his ears,

And then a word he finally spoke
Renewing all my fears.

He asked if I might offer him
Before I would be gone,
A drink to satisfy his thirst
From what I had just drawn.

Surprised that he would speak to me,
And more for what he pled,
I looked at him more closely there
And curious, then I said,

"Now please explain just how, kind sir,
You make of me this plea,
For Jews have no communion with
Samaritans like me."

I thought he was a bit ill-bred,
Or had it slipped his mind?
I'd put him in his place and hoped
He'd then his manners find.

But if his words surprised me what
He next said calm and clear
Resounded in my hearing and
Touched something deep and dear.

He spoke of living waters that,
Were his to offer free,
And if of him I asked for them
They would be given me.

And I, confused, then wondered what
These living waters were.

My heart beat hard as I gave thought
To what he might refer.

For there were things that I had done,
In truth, that I still did,
Quite known within my modest town,
And yet I wished them hid.

I thought it best to question who
This cryptic man might be.
Was Jacob lesser than this man
Now thought himself to be?

And how he would such waters give
Without the means at hand
With which to draw the waters out
From deep inside the land.

He heeded not but once again
Of living waters spoke.
These waters were a different kind, –
And hope within awoke!

He promised that his waters could
For those who would partake,
Spring up to life eternal and
Their thirst forever slake.

And still with understanding dim
I asked him for the gift,
That to this well I need not come,
Nor heavy buckets lift.

But then so strange, he asked of me
That I my husband seek.

And why, I thought, would he ask this,
And to my husband speak?

And so 'twas clear, he was not through,
Pursuing all the way,
Just what my life revealed and
Just what I had to say.

Since truth he sought I'd tell him that
I had no husband then,
And when he heard he answered thus,
"But you have had five men.

"And he who shares your home with you
Is not your husband now."
And hardly I believed my ears
Or that he knew somehow.

A word of kindness then he spoke
As if commending me,
That I claimed not a husband but
Had spoken truthfully.

And though at first I thought he was
A common Jew at best,
I now believed he was much more
As his words would attest.

A prophet, then? Perchance he was,
But still of Jewish root.
The mountain where we worshipped they
Were zealous to dispute.

And once again pursuing truth
He touched my greatest need,

Revealing how my soul might be
From all its bondage freed.

He spoke not of Jerusalem
But of a Father who
Sought worshippers who offered praise
In spirit and were true.

It mattered not the place he said,
For God a spirit is,
And Jew or other worshipping
In truth this way are his.

And with such thoughts invading me
And reaching every part
Of my base soul and mind and to
The depths of my poor heart,

With one last word in hopes I could
Suppress the light within
That shone more brightly as he spoke
Revealing all my sin,

"I know," I said, "Messiah comes,
Foretold so long ago,
And then to us he will explain
And all things will we know."

But my discomfort ended not,
Which I had hoped to see.
"In truth he comes," the stranger said,
"For I who speak am he."

And with that word so confident,
So calmly said to me,

I felt at last I knew just who
This stranger had to be.

And all my longings and my hopes,
And all my guilt and sin,
Then in a sudden, furious swell
Came surging from within.

He was the One I'd hoped for long!
He was the promised Christ!
Of woman born, the prophets wrote,
And for us sacrificed.

And then I understood just why
My life he sought to bare,
It was to show how great my need
For him who thirsted there.

And leaving then my jug with him
As friends of his arrived,
I hurry to my village now,
My heart and soul revived!

For many there, both friends and kin,
I know have equal pain,
And how I long to help each one
This new found joy to gain!

I'll share with them just what I learned
While talking with this man,
And who I found him then to be,
And how it all began.

A Widow from Nain

(Lk. 7)

The gates seem darker on this day
As slowly we pass through,
And not as wide as I had thought
Nor friendly as I knew.

We leave the city walls behind,
And I, surrounded by
This crowd of mourners yet alone,
Breathe pain with every sigh.

And yonder hill is where we'll pause
To bury this dear son.
Our first, our only son was he
And now I'm left with none.

His father there has found his rest
In dark, eternal sleep.
I'll lay my son beside his grave
And henceforth doubly weep.

And kindness now is shown by those
Who walk with me this day.
They offer words of sympathy
And some will even pray.

But shortly I'll be out of mind
When distant from their gaze.

They'll turn to cares more closely found,
  And go about their ways.

Does God indeed behold this day
  All that my heart endures?
Does he the hopeless, helpless view
  And then his aid bestirs?

No answer has he given me
  Though I have pondered well.
'Tis best I bury, mourn and then
  Begin my life of hell.

Ahead! I see a crowd that comes,
  A tumult ventures nigh.
And will my suff'ring be prolonged
  As they come tramping by?

Or will the coffin borne aloft
  Some deference invoke,
Though well they'll see its wooden frame
  Is pine and not of oak.

What's that? They've stopped! A man comes forth,
  He's set on me his eye,
And now beside the coffin says,
  "Good woman, don't you cry."

A smile I see, the only one
  Within the crowd around,
But in those words he gently spoke
  A trace of love I found.

And turning to the coffin then,
  Wherein the body lies,

"Young man!" he says addressing him,
　"I say to you – arise!"

And knows he not, this stranger bold
　Surrounded by a crowd,
That 'tis my son, my only, there
　In death's bedarkened shroud?

But rising then from death's cold grip,
　My son I see alive!
For death its claim could not maintain
　Nor of his life deprive.

I hear him speak but understand
　Not what he says for joy
That fills my heart as I behold
　My life, my hope, my boy!

And then this stranger bolder yet,
　Clasps gently by the hand
My son and leads him to the place
　Where I in wonder stand.

The voices now proclaim as one,
　"A prophet has appeared.
Our God once more his mercy shows,
　His people, has endeared!"

I know not who the stranger is
　But still he leaves this sign,
That in his smile the joy I see
　Is greater far than mine.

A Sinful Woman

(Lk. 7)

My name was known throughout the town
For I was thought to be
A woman of the night and thus
Of dubious pedigree.

But none had ever cared to learn
Or hear my saddened tale,
'Mongst women of the better class
Or less the highborn male.

And my allurements drew all types,
My craft the lot did span,
For little faith in God I held
And none I had in man.

But as the years came one by one
And clients by the drove,
Within I sensed discord somehow,
No matter how I strove.

No satisfaction did I gain,
Nor did my sorrow ease.
An emptiness was all I knew
That nothing could appease.

And then I heard of Jesus when
A man I once had met

Appeared and said goodbye for good,
And cancelled all his debt.

His life had taken quite a turn
He said and offered proof,
No more would he be found again
'Neath my or other's roof.

Yes God he said was in that man
Who sinners came to save,
Who preached and healed and demons cast
But most of all forgave.

And shortly would I hear of him
From others all around,
Who also had his call obeyed
And what they sought they found.

My soul then longed to meet him and
To know if it were true,
What I was hearing daily and
If he could love me too.

I'd met him not nor seen him though
His likeness dwelt in those
Who heard his call to follow him
And life with him then chose.

A love for him was born in me
But brought scant joy because
The more I loved, the more my shame
For all I'd done – and was.

But when he was invited by
A Pharisee to dine,

I rose and hurried to the place
And saw him there recline.

The Pharisee would have no use
For me in any way.
I knew a welcome waited not
On this or any day.

But this was not just any day
For Jesus was inside!
I thought if I but heard his voice,
Content I would abide.

I slipped beyond the door and there
I stood close by his feet,
And listened to each word he spoke
As they began to eat.

And soon my eyes were moist with tears,
With all its shame my heart
Seemed crushed but only that he might
New life to me impart.

He spoke and love itself distilled,
His radiance filled the air,
And soon I knelt to kiss his feet
And wipe them with my hair.

A jar of rare perfume I had
And poured it lavishly,
But hardly was its scent perceived
In his sweet company.

And soon the conversation turned
And Jesus spoke of two

Who owed a lender money but
Had none for what was due.

The lender knew their circumstance,
To sue them he was loath,
And so in kindness he declared
He would forgive them both.

Now I that debtor was who owed
The greater sum, 'twas clear,
But then this word of comfort came
Quite meant for me to hear.

"In those whom God forgives the most,
More love for him is born,
But little love dwells in those who
For sin are not forlorn.

"And Simon," Jesus then declared,
"I have this word for you,
No water you provided for
My feet as good hosts do.

"Yet she my feet has moistened with
Her very tears here shed,
And kissed and then anointed them
With sweet perfume instead.

"And thus I tell you that her sins
I freely now forgive,
And cancel all her debt that she
Henceforth in peace might live."

And then he spoke those very words
To my most shattered soul,

And I have ever followed since
That day he made me whole.

Now oft I've asked whence came such gall,
What power my actions bid,
That to old Simon's house I'd go
And weep the way I did.

For like a noisome guest was I,
And hardly like a wraith,
But deep within I trusted him
And Jesus called it faith.

A Woman Healed

(Lk. 8)

She suffered much through many a year,
A dozen now without relief,
And doctors, 'spite the sums she spent,
Could not allay her grief.

The more she saw of them the worse
Her constant flow of blood became,
Which of their honor spoke not well
But rather of their shame.

And then one day a man passed by,
She'd heard he cared for those in need.
No doctor he, but able still
A plaintive voice to heed.

But such the crush around him that
To speak a word of her affair
She knew would not be possible,
That he might be aware.

And thinking more of all she'd heard
Of how he loved, forgave and healed,
She chose her shyness to deny
And to her hopes then yield.

"I need but touch his garment and
This illness shall depart from me."

And with these words she stole ahead,
In fear yet hopefully.

'Twas but the slightest touch he felt
From this poor woman's weakened hand,
Yet such the power that from him flowed
No illness could withstand.

And in that moment she was healed,
Renewed in spirit and in soul,
Her years of suffering finally past,
Her body now made whole.

Then Jesus turned to view the crowd
And asked who touched him 'mongst them all,
For power he said had flowed through him
To meet some forlorn call.

And she, now freed of all but fear,
With lips and knees aquiver there,
Stepped forth in answer to his plea,
Her happy tale to share.

"My daughter, go in peace," he said,
"And from your suffering be freed.
Your faith has proved sufficient for
Your soul and body's need."

A Canaanite Woman

(Mat. 15)

For long I'd wondered when her voice
Like some sweet, welcome melody,
Might greet these ears so sorrow-filled,
Their anguish turn to ecstasy,

Or that her tongue unloosed for once,
Might send aloft some reasoned phrase
That set upon each listener well,
To finally end the skeptic's gaze.

For demons had possessed this child,
This much beloved daughter mine,
And daily as she grew the worse
My hopes but lingered in decline.

She suffered much in throes of fit,
And deeply scarred my heart knew not
Just where some help I might yet gain
That I had not already got.

I chanced to hear one day a word
That friend to friend then passed along.
It told there was a prophet nigh
Who turned deep mourning into song.

'Mongst Jewish people he was born,
Of late had come good news to share.

But I though Greek still thought perhaps
He'd hear my tear-filled plea and care.

The throng around him parted not,
    I was unwelcome by their kind,
    But hearts aflame with urgency
Are not by human will confined.

I cried aloud, "My daughter, Lord,
From demons suffers night and day.
    Have mercy, Son of David, and
Some kind and healing word now say."

    But not a word he said. Was I
    To take this silence and return?
    No, yet again I loud implored
    That I some benefit might earn.

What other hope remained to me?
    But as my pleadings I would urge,
His followers spoke, commanding me
    To stop my most unwelcome dirge.

And once again I thought 'twas true,
Few men would hear and fewer heed
    Or understand a mother's heart
For any daughter found in need.

And then he spoke this solemn word
    Which hardly satisfied my soul,
That serving Israel's poor lost sheep
Fulfilled his work in part and whole.

    And quickly then I knelt before
    This cryptic man of noble mien,

Imploring that he heal my child
And end this troubling, frightful scene.

And once again he answered me,
Though not as if to heed my cry,
"The children's bread should not be cast
To dogs that 'neath the table lie."

'Twas rightly said I knew at once,
And meekly then I answered, "Sir,
The crumbs that from the table fall
Will quite suffice a hungry cur."

"How great your faith, dear woman! Now,
Your plea in full is granted you!"
And hurriedly I took my leave
Not daring to believe 'twas true.

And as my humble cottage door
I opened, there to see or hear
My daughter's sad condition and
Just how to me she might appear,

A voice I heard so clear, so sweet,
"Oh, mother dear, you've come at last.
For long I'd waited 'midst a dream,
And all my darkness now is past."

Let Him Be the First

(Jno. 8)

At dawn they brought her spitefully,
Without regard for love or pride,
And deepest pain she humbly bore
Which neither guilt nor shame could hide.

They made her stand midst all the crowd,
Assembled well and anxious each,
For early Jesus had arrived
God's love and mercy there to teach.

Now experts in the Law were they,
And Pharisees with one intent,
To trap him in his words and thus
Some false or legal charge invent.

They cited well their ancient Law,
That sinners in the very act,
And caught without excuse or doubt
Should die without delay in fact.

"Now say to us what should be done
The Law's requirement to secure?"
They posed the question hoping well
He'd give his answer nor demur.

But Jesus bent and on the ground
Most cryptically began to write,

Nor did he answer yet a word
To clear the woman or indict.

And finally when they pressed him hard
He stood and acquiescing said,
"Let him now free of sin begin,
And cast the first stone at her head."

And kneeling then once more he wrote,
His finger tracing on the ground,
As one and all the men gave thought
If worthy any might be found.

Now silence reigned until a man
With agile hand and ready stone,
Quite harmlessly then let it fall
And walked away, head bowed, alone.

And then there followed one by one,
Till all were gone most deeply shamed,
From eldest to the youngest man
With all their righteous zeal tamed.

"Now where are those who would condemn?"
Asked Jesus as he stood and spoke.
"Do none deserving count themselves
Their lawful sentence to invoke?"

And then for once, her face aloft,
The woman spoke and gave reply.
"No man 'mongst these has yet remained
His harsh decree to justify."

"Nor shall I now condemn you for
The life you've lived," our Lord then said.

"Now go and leave your life of sin,
Pursuing better things instead."

And was it names of women that
In temple sands were written clear?
Or deeds, perhaps, the men had done
That hardened consciences would sear?

We know not nor shall ever know
But this at greatest peril forget,
Where men would judge and then condemn,
With God there is forgiveness yet.

Martha

Now Martha was upset because
The guests were all at hand,
And Mary was not helping so
If he would just command,

That's all the help she'd need right then
To serve them all their food,
To satisfy their cravings and
To set in jovial mood.

But Mary was quite disinclined
Or else she plain forgot.
She left it all to her poor sis
To serve the hungry lot.

And Martha had not failed to give
Her sister with an eye
A beckon to rise up and help,
But Mary chose to lie,

At Jesus' feet to hear him speak,
And ponder well and deep.
Her only wish, those quickening words
To treasure and to keep.

So Martha thought the time had come,
She'd speak to Jesus now.

She ventured near to where he stood
And with a dainty bow,

"My Lord," she said, "Do you not care
I'm working all alone?
Please tell my sister Mary there,
In calm and quiet tone,

"To come into the kitchen and
To lend a hand or two.
The people are awaitin' and
The laborers are few."

Now Jesus knew just what she faced,
He knew it all along.
He knew the work was heavy and
He knew there was a throng.

But also there were other things
He knew one need attend.
He wished not to deny her choice
Nor Mary's hope offend.

And so he said to Martha that
Too many things she'd let
Cause her to worry needlessly
And her dear soul upset.

And thus he showed 'twas not alone
Her interest in the meal,
But quite a lot of other things
She'd sought with too much zeal.

And then he said, "There's just one thing
That really matters much.

It's more important than all else
Like serving food and such.

"And Mary," he went on to say,
"Has seen something you've not.
For she has made a choice this night
And this great truth has caught,

"She's chosen at my feet to sit
And hear the words I speak,
For well she knows apart from me
How void her life and weak."

And so the meal was served, no doubt
A bit too cold and late,
For one can hardly serve a host
On time without a mate.

But if his words to Martha dear
To us seem somewhat stern,
It's for the truth these sisters show
That he would have us learn.

And I will say how much to me
These words of late have meant.
When bothered by too many things
A prayer of thanks I've sent,

Rememb'ring that one thing alone
Is all he wants from me.
It's not too different from that day
When Martha made her plea.

For he is still the Teacher and
He offers yet today

The chance to sit and learn from him,
  And all who wish to may.

And this I've learned as well from him
  That all who make this choice,
Will find there is no power on earth
  Can take away his voice.

A Secret Long Pursued

How strangely weak his followers were,
Enduring not in trial,
And ready soon to quit the fight
Nor walk the second mile.

This parable then Jesus gave
That they might always strive
In prayer to God who ever seeks
Our spirits to revive.

A certain judge who feared not God
Nor cared for man's estate,
Was daily by a widow vexed,
At dawn, noontide and late.

"Now grant me justice," was her plea,
"Against my lawless foe,
And my condition please review,
Some retribution show."

And for a while his ear was deaf
To all her urgency,
For naught he cared of God or man
And less this widow's plea.

But then the day arrived when he,
His patience at an end,

And near exhaustion turned about
Her pleading to attend.

"Unless I hear this woman's case
She'll not her suit forego.
She'll hound me to a certain death
And peace I'll never know."

And Jesus paused a moment then,
And to his followers said,
"Now hear this unjust man's reply
To what the woman pled.

"And will not God so caring and
So just in all his ways
Be quick to hear his chosen ones
Who call throughout their days,

"For justice 'gainst their enemies
And those who do them wrong?
Will he not swiftly judgment bring,
Nor pause nor tarry long?

"For God, unlike this spiteful judge,
The lowly stoops to hear,
Delighting when they raise their voice
To lend his kindly ear."

And with this final word the Lord
To every listener there
Revealed the secret, long pursued,
For God to answer prayer.

"And when the Son of Man," he said,
"Appears on earth again,

Will he though searching far and wide
Find faith among all men?"

This Favor over All

(Jno. 2; Mat. 21)

I early rise this misty dawn
And wake my children from their sleep,
That to the temple we may haste,
Our vigil there to keep.

An hour spent in prayer with God
Begins our harried day so well,
And hope we gain to do his will
And in his presence dwell.

Now countless are the times that hour
Ere I had risen to depart
Removed the pain and burdens from
My sad, despairing heart.

And would another hour or two
I had to kneel and linger there,
To sing, to praise or simply wait
Most quietly in prayer.

But widows must the time redeem
And vigilantly search each day,
That food for children's stomachs might
Be found and served some way.

But 'twas not always that we came
And found a corner calm, serene,

Where mother, son and daughter could
A moment's blessing glean.

For once within the temple courts
A desecrating mess was found,
With money changers at their seats
And birds and beasts around.

And merchants called as I my way
Would wend in hopes to pass them by.
They offered cattle, lamb or sheep
And for my coin would cry.

And such the raucous, hawking noise,
As they their profane wares would laud,
Quite hopeless was my quest to find
A tranquil place with God.

How much I owe that man who came
And raised his voice for what he saw,
And with a fashioned whip in hand
Put each of them in awe.

For as his whip upon their backs
Brought anguished cries of pain and woe,
They scurried from the presence of
That angry, violent foe.

He routed money changers and
Their laden tables overturned,
And none had courage to oppose
For well his wrath they earned.

"This house a house of prayer shall be
As once my Father did avow,

And not a den of robbers as
Your deeds have made it now!"

And with these words he drove them out,
Nor have they dared return as yet,
Such zeal consumed him for God's house
He thus their deeds beset.

Now many a day I've thought of him
For word of other signs is told,
As he among our people dwells
And they his works behold.

Much good he's done in every way,
But I this favor over all
Will cherish well beyond each one
As on the Lord I call,

Within the temple's quiet gates
Where once again on holy sod,
With humble praise and thankful heart
I seek and find my God.

Two Coins I Bring

(Mk. 12)

Two coins I bring, 'tis all I have,
Close held against my breast,
While others bear their sacks of gold
And fill the treasure chest.

Does God make note of offerings
As I this day will make,
Or do the rich alone deserve
His pleasure to partake?

And does God know how oft' I've longed
That I might worthily
A temple off'ring dedicate,
On humble, bended knee?

A widow, childless and alone
With scarce a mite to spend,
Yet still a meager gift I'll leave
In hopes I not offend,

E'en though the coin that's faintly heard
As I release my hold
Will little mean and little count,
Nor have its story told.

And shame I feel for what I give
But not to give is worse.

Can God somehow behold and grant
A blessing, not a curse?

And with the morrow I'll have need
A bit of food to buy.
A coin I'll leave, the other keep
My needs to satisfy.

But as I near the temple chest
A surge of love I feel,
For him who ever faithful is
Nor does his care conceal.

And quickly then I drop them both,
My heart allows no less,
The morrow will itself suffice,
Reprove me or will bless.

What's that I see? A man who smiles,
And surely he did see
As I so quickly dropped my coins
And turned about to flee.

He follows with his gaze until
His eye then catches mine,
And in that instant I perceive
A sense of the divine.

And somehow in that smile I knew
God saw and then was pleased.
He welcomed yet the smallest boon
And all my doubts appeased.

I leave the temple grounds my purse
A void between its seams,

But in my soul a peace prevails
And wealth beyond my dreams.

Her Only Treasure

(Mat. 26)

An alabaster jar quite filled
With aromatic, sweet perfume,
Enough to waft its scent afar
And fill a spacious room,

She brought with her e'en though it was
The only treasure she might claim.
No other thought would she allow,
A lesser gift would shame.

She boldly entered Simon's house
Who once from leprosy was cured,
And likely by his honored guest
Who spoke a healing word.

She saw him there reclining 'midst
The many who had come to dine,
And bolder still, she ventured forth
As food was served and wine.

She broke the vessel and outflowed
The soft and liquid purplish balm
Whose fragrance was like nectar that
Should every bother calm.

His hair was moistened well throughout
As down the snarled locks it flowed,

And soon the rich aroma filled
Old Simon's bright abode.

But some there were offended by
This costly unguent on his head.
"What waste! You could have sold the jar
And helped the poor!" they said.

And chiding thus they thought to put
The woman rudely in her place,
But Jesus finally spoke these words
Her kindness to embrace,

"Why trouble her for what she's done?
The poor you ever have and may
At your convenience give to them
Fulfilling what you say.

"The thing she's done to me this day
Is beautiful beyond compare,
And shortly I will take my leave,
You'll know not when or where.

"To ready me for what ahead
My soul forebodingly awaits,
My body she anointed thus
To meet death's looming gates.

"And truthfully I tell you now
In lands close by or far afield,
Where'er the gospel may be preached
Her deed will be revealed."

Mary Magdalene

(Lk. 8; Jno. 20)

I followed him where'er he went
That I might hear him speak,
Through desert, coastland, open plain,
On windswept mountain peak.

I followed him in whom my hopes
Were born anew one day,
When by a single word he cast
A demon host away.

Yes, seven had indwelt me then,
Tormenting day and night,
And warring 'gainst my better will
Left naught but grief and blight.

But when in mercy he removed
That darkened, deathly veil,
Such light infused my clouded soul,
I vowed and would not fail,

I'd serve his needs with what I had
And join with others who
Had confidently heard his word,
And found it sure and true.

So other women then I found
About as poor as I,

But somehow from our means his needs
We hoped we could supply.

And Jesus had for each of us
His noble mercy shown,
While such concern for women was
Among our men unknown.

We traveled much for Jesus said
Whate'er you sow you reap,
And thus he sought to bring God's word
To Israel's poor lost sheep.

And with him his apostles went,
The twelve he chose so well,
Though one who later turned on him
Has earned his place in hell.

They often found no place to stay
And were received so rude,
But from our meager means we gave
Sufficient drink and food.

I saw him take upon himself
The sickness others had.
A widow lost her only son
But he restored the lad.

A tax collector served a meal
Within his sumptuous place,
And hearing Jesus' words he chose
Salvation to embrace.

And sinners had their sins forgiv'n
While others were denied,

The former for their penitence,
The others for their pride.

He spoke with clear authority
Unlike the priests today,
And those with hunger in their hearts
Went satisfied away.

A woman from a foreign land
One day her faith revealed,
And then her daughter demon-owned,
Was from her illness healed.

He told us much of heav'n and hell.
The narrow gate, he said,
Alone will bear us heavenward
When finally we are dead.

And even more there is to say
Of how he lived and taught.
There's much I've yet to follow in
And much that I forgot.

'Twas from a distance there we viewed,
(And this I'll not forget),
As on a cross he hung one day,
The end, we feared, he'd met.

We wondered then, my friends and I,
Just where his followers were,
And why those dozen men of his
Did not themselves bestir.

For not a one of them was found
Who stood there by his side.

They ran or watched him quietly
Until he finally died.

I saw where he was laid that day
Within a chilly cave,
A rocky shelter freshly carved,
But not a worthy grave.

And on the third day following,
Quite early in the morn,
Some friends and I took spices there,
Still grieving and forlorn.

We found the stone was rolled away,
We never knew by whom,
And looking in we saw him not
Within that empty tomb.

And staying on a while alone
In tears, my heart was torn.
I knew not of his whereabouts
Nor where his body borne.

But suddenly, I can't explain,
A presence I perceived.
I turned and saw this man who was
The gardener, I believed.

"Dear woman, why these tears?" he said,
"And whom do you now seek?"
So gentle were his words to me
I ventured then to speak,

"Oh sir," I said, imploring him,
"If you have borne him hence,

Please tell me where you've laid him now
And I will fetch him thence."

And then he spoke my name as did
That Man I'd followed years.
'Twas Jesus stood before me there
And gone were all my tears!

He spoke my name but once before
Straight to his side I flew.
"Oh, teacher!" then I said to him,
"Oh, teacher, it is you!"

He wished not that I hold him close
For he had yet to rise,
And in his Father's presence dwell,
Ascending through the skies.

"But go," he said, "my brothers tell,
To each who now despairs,
That to my Father I return,
To my God and to theirs."

And then without delay I searched
And finding them I said,
"I saw and spoke with Jesus for
He's risen from the dead!

"He called me by my name and then
I held him to my breast."
But when his followers heard my words
They thought I spoke in jest.

Now Peter had a bit more faith,
(Though sometimes not a lot),

With John he ran to see if I
Had told the truth or not.

And now we wait for their return,
They'll tell us what they see.
They thought my words had little worth
Just as they've thought of me.

But whether then, they will affirm
That Jesus is alive,
Or harshly censure all I've said
When finally they arrive,

If you would ask of this poor maid
Just why my life has worth,
It's that I've found no greater love
Than his in all the earth.

Pilate's Wife

(Mat. 27)

I dreamed a dream of justice ere
I rose to greet this troubled day,
And since, there's not a moment come
My troubled temper to allay.

A man of whom I'd heard good things
And on occasion witnessed too,
Was now before the tribunal
There to receive some judgment due.

I saw him early in my dream
Surrounded by a surly crowd,
That cared not for a widow's plight
But all his praises sang aloud.

He stopped and turning looked at her,
She suffered much some malady,
Which to each doctor she had seen
Remained as yet a mystery.

She touched his garment with her hand,
Quite withered and devoid of strength,
And felt at once her body healed
Throughout its wizened, frail length.

A father with his wife implored
He raise their daughter from the sleep

That finally comes upon us all
Nor does for children favor keep.

He took her lifeless hand and spoke
In words her mother oft had said
When calling her to greet the morn,
And then he raised her from the dead.

And this was he whom priests accused?
'Twas this man's life they now pursued?
Yet more my troubled dream declared
Before its content I conclude.

His followers were as poor as he
And on a Sabbath gathered grain,
Though well they knew on such a day
Their Law enjoined them to abstain.

Then leaders of their sect, outraged,
Brought accusations 'gainst them all,
As if their deed were quite severe
And not to be considered small.

But Jesus did what no man dared
Defending them and even more,
He justified their actions by
Reciting deeds of men of lore.

And then my dream brought clear to mind
What others had related well,
Of how this man his taxes paid
Nor from such duties would rebel.

"To Caesar render all," he said,
"That to him rightly may pertain,

Nor fail to offer God his due
Whate'er it be in his domain."

We ruled with justice, firm, severe,
And all our laws its nature mirrored.
Lament the man condemned thereby,
For every Jew our sentence feared.

And thus the innocent we've kept
From condemnation undeserved,
Much pride we take that in our courts
The innocent are thus preserved.

And then the more my dream transpired
The more my sense of shame increased.
Within our land this man though Jew,
Would know a cross till life had ceased.

His enemies were ours I thought,
His friends, the poor who kept their place.
And what was there for me to do
That I myself each day could face?

My dream is now some hours past,
But every passion it awoke
Most loudly pleads I find some way
That I just sentence may invoke.

***

"Dear husband, find within your heart
Some pardon for my boldness now,
For I have never thought to say
What judgments you should make or how.

"But on this very day by morn
I suffered much within a dream,
For him who stands before the throne
On specious charges, it would seem.

"Much thought I've taken ere this note
I dared to write and more to send,
But finally knew I must find peace
And all my inner turmoil end.

"Accept, dear husband, this advice
Which by my trembling hand I've sent.
Have naught to do with Jesus for
Of every charge he's innocent."

Peter's Wife

(Mat. 8)

Most silently I wait this morn,
A sickly mother by my side,
While thoughts continue e'er to roam
O'er past misfortunes that abide.

No man shall come when falls the night
Assuring a warm fire's blaze
Within our cottage walls made bright,
On which contentedly we gaze.

And this shall be but one more night
Of waiting in uncertainty
For him who three years past took flight,
And ended our felicity.

E'er since he heard a call that day
From one he met beside the shore,
He's seldom home and oft away
Though I his presence yet implore.

Some gift from heav'n he says is vowed
To those who followed o'er each trail,
And now as one, in prayer and bowed,
They hope some blessing to avail.

Who is this man he followed so,
Whose prayers it seemed reached to the skies?

And why was Peter set to go
Wherever Jesus turned his eyes?

I met him on a busy day
When Peter brought him to our place.
My mother with a fever lay
And I cared not this man to face.

We had but little wine and bread,
And mother's fever naught would quell.
He saw her lying in the bed
And with a touch he made her well!

Had I then judged him quite amiss?
Had Peter made some happy choice?
Could I my fearfulness dismiss?
Would we one day for him rejoice?

And as the days, nay years then passed
I heard from Peter more accounts
Of healings and of demons cast
That to this day all faith surmounts.

I questioned if my Peter then,
Had gone too far in his belief.
He's had sharp words with many men
But has survived, to my relief!

And while they wait for heaven's gift
I'll tell you now of further things.
There was a time when deep adrift
And every man to something clings,

This Jesus walked upon the sea,
And Peter, bless him, then was moved

To make of Jesus this strange plea,
To likewise walk that faith be proved.

And I was horrified to hear
My husband so disdained his life,
That he would such a fool appear
And make yet poorer his dear wife.

For often have I wondered whence
Might come the morrow's fish or fruit,
It's added much to my suspense
And made distress yet more acute.

But this I'll say with little fear
Of contradiction or dispute,
A change in Peter, sweet and clear,
I saw in him as in pursuit

Of Jesus he marched on each day,
And oft was taken to the side,
To learn yet more of how to pray
That in God's ways he should abide.

But was it all, I ask, in vain?
For but two months ago there came
A change of mood I can't explain
That brought to Jesus lowest shame.

They tried him and condemned there,
They saw him die upon a cross,
They heard him breathe a final prayer
Nor thought his death would be their loss.

And strangest of all things till now
About this strangest man 'mongst men,

My Peter did to me avow,
He saw him raised to life again!

My bones! How weary as I wait!
What's that?! Some loud commotion stirs,
And people running as if fate
Has beckoned and each heart concurs.

And will this noisome crowd be heard
By Peter and his friends who wait?
Will God's vowed gift now be conferred,
Or must this bedlam first abate?

A sound of rushing wind I hear
And people shouting to be heard,
While words quite foreign reach my ear
And men inquire, "What has occurred?"

My way to Peter I've begun,
And will he rue this futile choice?
But now I hear the speech of one...
Hark! How it sounds like Peter's voice!

Lydia's Quest

(Acts 16)

In Thyatira I was born
Of parents finely clad,
I wanted naught within our home
For all the care I had.

The servants who attended me
Foresaw each wish or need,
And quickly moved at my behest
Each childish plea to heed.

And growing up in luxury
With all I had to boast,
I knew o'er time I something lacked,
And that I wanted most.

And thus there came the day when I
A merchant then became,
A clothier in rich purple things
For wealthy men of fame.

Yes kings, I thought, would wear my cloth,
Bestrewn with flecks of gold,
And royal lips would speak my name
As honored ones of old.

I traded well, my cloth was known
And everywhere admired.

I found at last the fame I'd sought
But not what I desired.

An emptiness still lingered near,
A hunger in my heart
That wealth or fame could not o'ercome
Or cause it to depart.

Now Philippi is where I lived
When all my wealth I gained,
And there I sought out friends to quell
The void that yet remained.

I found them, women of my class,
Of stock renowned and fine,
Whose lives were filled with pleasures and
Were barren just like mine.

And this I found as well with them,
The women who had most,
Were those who midst their affluence
Least happiness could boast.

And then it seemed I'd sought amiss
For happiness within,
And gave a thought to others who
Believed in God and sin.

I turned to those whose history
Was known in every place,
To Jews who worshipped God above
And were his chosen race.

So I became a "worshipper"
Of him they called the Lord.

From hunger had I searched and found,
And this was my reward.

But over time—it took not long -
I found I wanted still,
For ever present was a void
This faith could not fulfill.

Or was it that the one true God
Of whom the Jews were heirs,
Was God indeed yet hidden by
The rituals which were theirs?

And so did I continue in
A life of wealth and ease,
In hopes of finding faith that would
My restless heart appease.

I passed some years and then one day
By river's side I heard
A man of meager circumstance
Who brought a certain word.

A peace, a joy, a confidence
I saw within his face,
As lingering, I finally learned
Of God's forgiving grace.

I knew at once he had what I
Had sought and never found,
And soon his message strong and clear
Within me would resound.

He spoke of Jesus, born a Jew,
Who had redeemed our race

By keeping all the Law and then
By dying in our place.

He spoke of life forgiven, free,
And by the Spirit led,
And nourished not by earthly goods
But by a heav'n-sent bread.

He spoke of hope awaiting us
When Jesus would return,
And said our life upon the earth
Is but a brief sojourn.

And then so clear it came to me
Why nothing had availed,
As I my empty heart had sought
For years to fill – but failed.

Yet all the while this God whom I
Could neither hear nor see,
Was following through my wasted path
And kindly guiding me.

To God I've given all I am
And all I have as well.
My home an open door shall have
Where friends may come and dwell.

My heart no longer pleads nor pines
And from my quest I'm free,
But little credit do I claim
For he, in truth, found me.

Priscilla's Tale

(Acts 18)

I fancied not that distant day
When first I hap'ly heard
From one whose name is long forgot,
This odd, perplexing word,

That God had sent a Savior who
Upon a cross of late,
Had suffered and redeemed us from
A just, deservéd fate.

And those who trusted him who died
Would life anew perceive,
As all his will they sought to keep
And to his teachings cleave.

I fancied not, I say, just what
This life they called The Way
Would mean in all its consequence
On that most fateful day.

But here I now recount this tale,
In brief, my friend, that you
May know just how my God has led
In paths e'er straight and true.

Now with my husband Aquila
I found myself in Rome.

Its grandeur took my breath away
And there we built a home.

But short indeed our stay for when
The Emperor gave command,
All Jews were ordered to depart
And seek another land.

To Corinth then we came and found
A lively group, I'd say,
Of those who also trusted God
And worshipped in their way.

And there a man had gone to preach
To whom an ample debt
I've owed since first I heard his voice,
The very day we met.

His name was Paul and God had called
This servant to his work,
Nor did he waver to obey
Nor any burden shirk.

Like us a maker of fine tents and so
We asked him to reside
With us a while within our home
And labor side by side.

And much I learned from this dear man
While working or at rest,
For he was specially ordained
God's truth to manifest.

So whether then while tending to
A needle, thread or hide,

Or sharing in a meal or yet
In prayer by river's side,

I sensed a heart so filled with love
It made his every word
As though from heav'n a call went forth,
And every doubt obscured.

A meeting place our home became
For others of The Way,
Where one might stop to rest a bit,
To find a meal or pray.

And once again our home we left
As with our brother Paul,
We journeyed on to Ephesus
Attending to God's call.

And there a learnéd man we met,
An Alexandrian Jew,
Who preached with fervor from the Word
And taught all that he knew.

Yet as we listened it was plain,
Repentance was his theme,
But not the cross of Jesus nor
Its power to redeem.

And so we took Apollos home
More fully to explain
Who Jesus was that he might then
A fuller knowledge gain.

And oh! What pleasure then was mine!
And how I would rejoice.

For Christians everywhere were blessed
As he in ardent voice,

Proclaimed the gospel hither, yon,
By God's most wondrous grace,
And aided many who believed,
Both Jew and pagan race.

We traveled much in serving God,
By dusty road and sea.
We met and worked with many saints
Including Timothy.

Our pathway was not always bright,
At times it seemed quite grim.
And more than once we risked our lives
For Paul, supporting him.

But following God with gladdened hearts
We were in turn well served
By many others of the faith,
Far more than we deserved.

Now looking back on all the things
That happened through the years,
Two persons stand above the rest
And bring me joyous tears.

For blessed we were in knowing Paul
Whose heart-felt prayers we heard,
Apollos too, who stirred our souls
Each time he spoke the Word.

And now, dear friend, I end my tale
Though yet there's much to say,

Of God and all his kindness as
We've walked his chosen way.